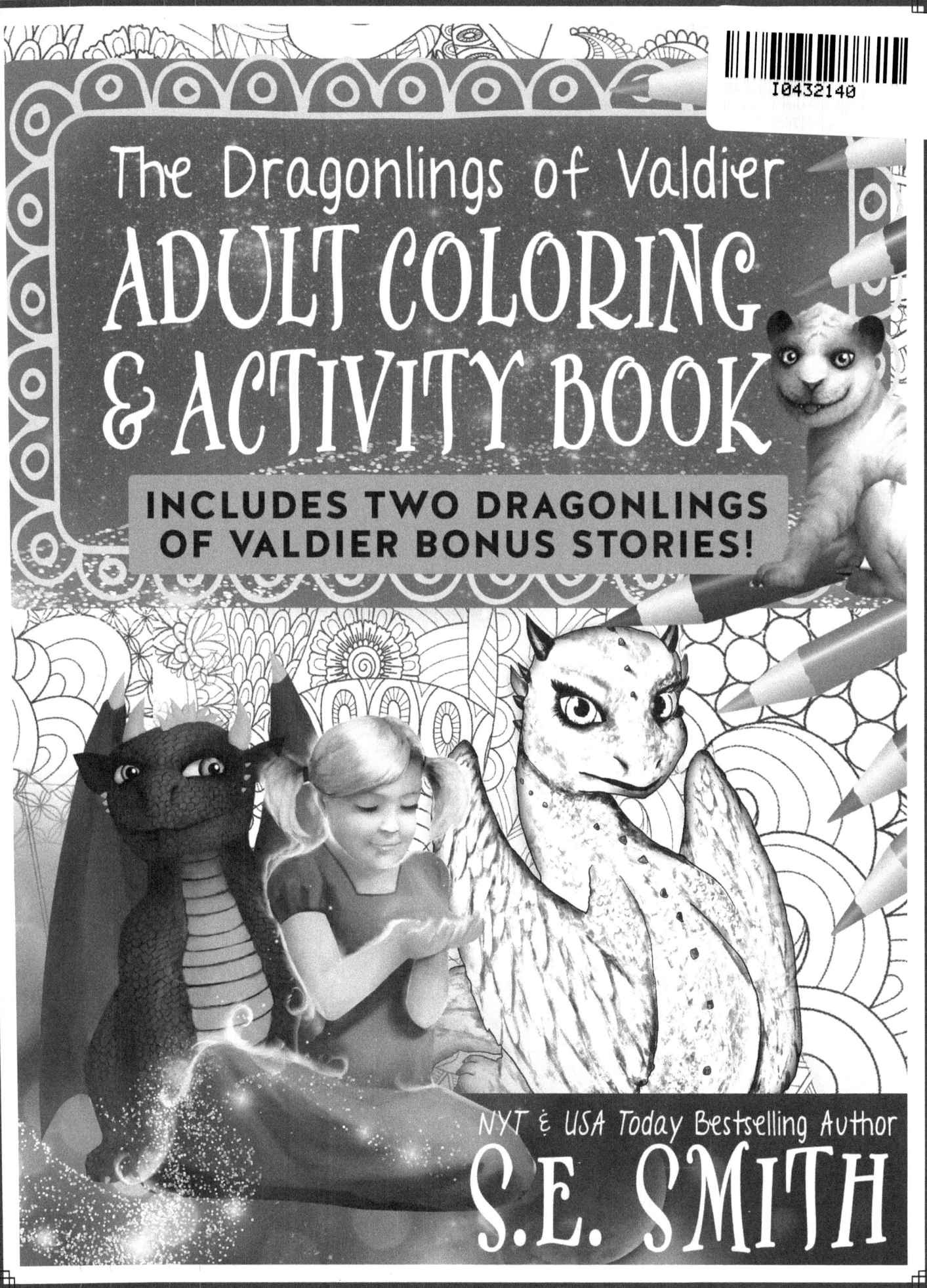

Science Fiction Romance
Dragonlings of Valdier Adult Coloring Book and Story
Copyright © 2018 by S.E. Smith
First E-Book Published February 2018
The Breakfast Run: A Dragonlings of Valdier Short Story
Copyright © 2016 by S.E. Smith
First E-book Published April 2016
Cover Design by Melody Simmons

ALL RIGHTS RESERVED: This literary work may not be reproduced or transmitted in any form or by any means, including electronic or photographic reproduction, in whole or in part, without express written permission from the author.

All characters, places, and events in this book are fictitious or have been used fictitiously, and are not to be construed as real. Any resemblance to actual persons living or dead, actual events, locales, or organizations are strictly coincidental and not intended by the author.

Summary: A quick trip to the village for breakfast turns into a hunt for two missing Dragonlings with their dad in hot pursuit! Who ever knew keeping track of a dragonling could be so much work? This book also contains an Adult Coloring book and games.

Published in the United States by Montana Publishing.

{1. Holiday – Fiction. 2. Paranormal Romance. – Fiction. 3. Action/Adventure – Fiction. 4. Fantasy – Fiction. 5. Science Fiction – Fiction 6. Shape shifters – Fiction}.}

ISBN: 978-1986043182 (Paperback)
ISBN: 978-1-944125-32-5 (eBook)

www.montanapublishinghouse.com

The Breakfast Run:
A Dragonlings of Valdier Short Story

By S.E. Smith

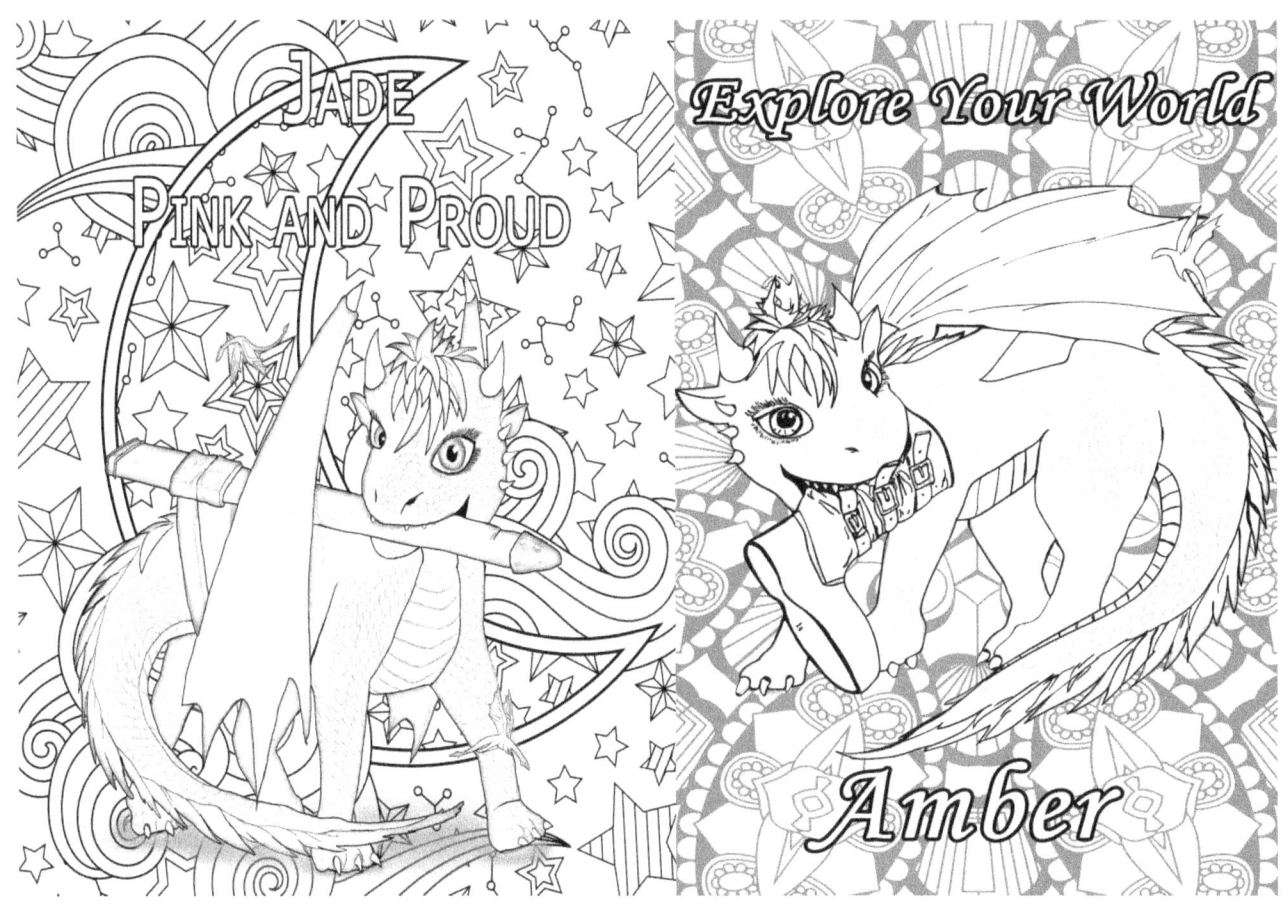

Trelon gazed around the market in panic. He couldn't believe he had lost the girls. All he could think of now was that Cara was going to kill him. Only last night he had bragged that he could handle them with one hand tied behind his back and his eyes closed! They were older now. He didn't have to worry about diapers and bottles anymore. Surely taking them to market to buy some fresh fruit and bread for breakfast wouldn't be that difficult. Cara did it all the time!

Turning in a circle, he groaned as his gaze swept the crowded street. Where were they?! It was supposed to be a quick, fun, easy trip. Go to the market, get something special for breakfast and get back before Cara even realized that they were gone.

"Do you see them?" Trelon asked Symba, his and Cara's symbiot in a low desperate voice. The large golden Werecat sneezed and shook its head. "You're no help! You know, she's going to blame you, too, if we don't find them."

Symba shivered and shook before a portion of the liquid gold body dissolved into a dozen tiny dragons. Trelon released a deep breath and nodded. This would allow them to expand their search.

"Good idea," Trelon muttered. "Go! Find them."

He watched as the tiny golden dragons took off through the crowd. Plastering a strained smile to his lips, he walked over to the merchant that he had been talking to a few moments ago. Swallowing, he opened his mouth to ask the merchant if he had perchance seen which way the girls had gone.

"They love colorful balls," the merchant stated before he even uttered a word.

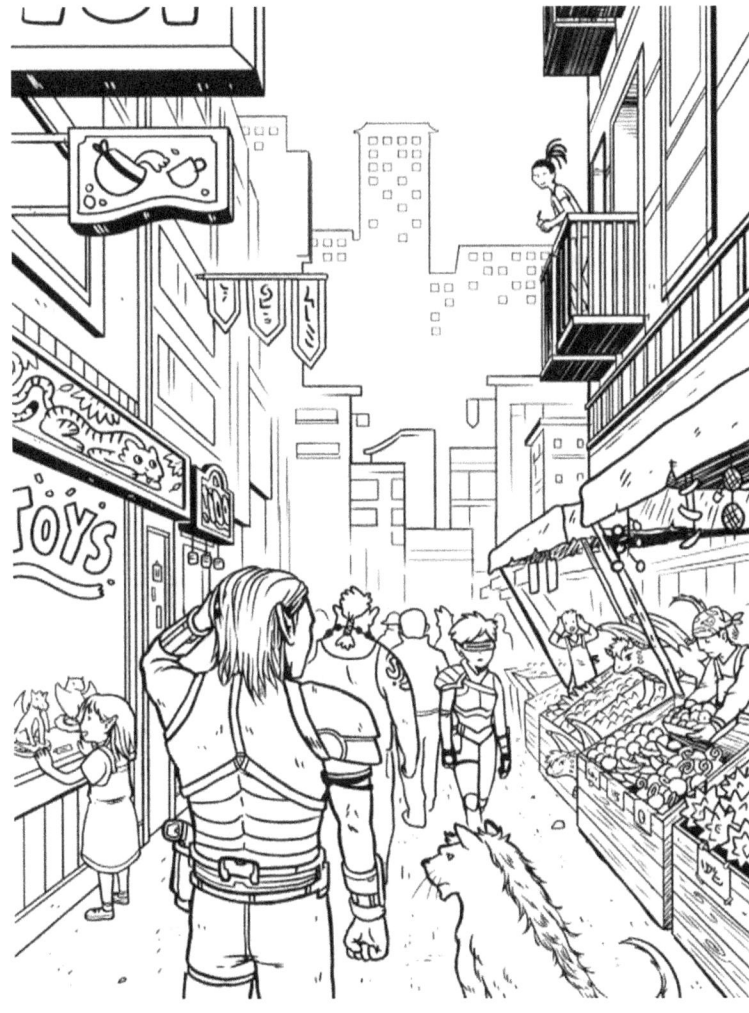

"The colorful balls?" Trelon asked in confusion.

"Cart 105, three carts down and on the left," the merchant chuckled. "Amber likes red, Jade likes pink, and Lady Cara likes them all."

Trelon did a double take when the merchant chuckled and pointed. With a nod, he turned and hurried through the crowds. He was almost to the merchant's stand when he heard a familiar squeal. Breathing a sigh of relief, he pushed through the crowd. Behind the stand was a large, circular bin filled with colorful balls. For a moment, Trelon had a feeling of déjà vu when he saw it. It reminded him of the ball pit Cara had created in the Haunted House playground under the palace.

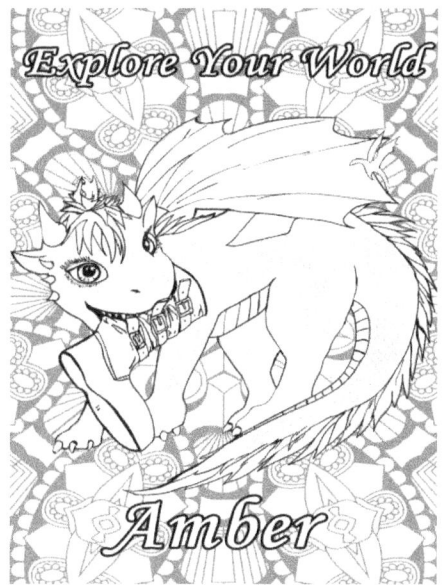

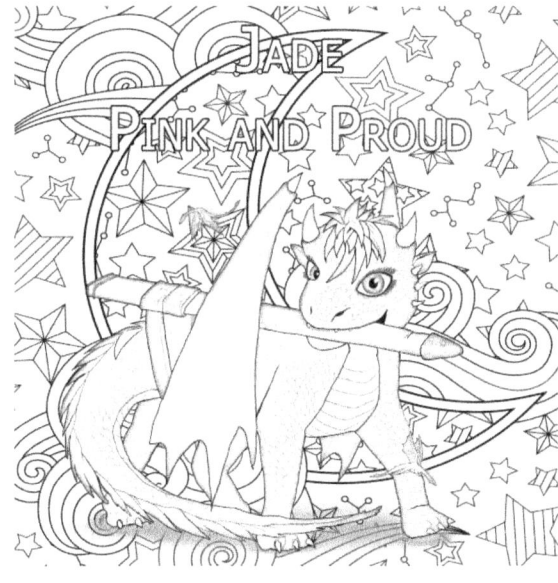

"Amber!" Trelon called out when he saw a tiny dragon's head pop up from under the balls. "Jade!"

Two sets of dark gold eyes peered back at him before disappearing beneath the colorful balls. With a soft growl, Trelon walked around the stand, tossing a coin onto the merchant's table. Sitting on the side, he lifted his legs over it and sank down into the pit. He grunted in surprise, not expecting it to come up to his waist.

"Girls, we've got to… ouch!" Trelon muttered, grabbing his butt. "Amber, no biting!"

"Dada, playtimes!" Jade giggled, coming up a few inches in front of him. "Catches me!"

Trelon groaned when Jade suddenly disappeared. "No's playtimes," he called, scrambling forward to grab Jade. "Where did you go?"

Trelon pushed at the colored balls, but as fast as he pushed them aside, more took their place. He twisted when he felt something brush against his leg. Reaching down, he grunted in triumph when his fingers wrapped around a tiny leg. Pulling it upward, the grin of delight faded to confusion when, instead of one of his daughters, he held the leg of a small boy.

"Let's me go!" The boy yelled, swinging out his tiny fist.

Trelon dropped the boy when the fist connected with the tip of his nose, sending burning tears to his eyes. He shook his head and watched in blurry astonishment as the little boy disappeared beneath the balls. Unease filled him when he felt several more bumps against his legs when he stumbled backwards. It took a moment to realize that the whole pit was alive with wiggling bodies.

Turning to climb out, Trelon's hand swept along his hip to wipe his suddenly sweaty palm down his leg. He paled when he felt the empty sheath. With a silent curse, he realized that he had lost his knife in the bubbling rainbow of balls. Glancing wildly around, he hoped that none of the little ones climbing in and out found it before he could.

Turning again, he dove head first into the round toys. He paused when the body of another little boy rolled past him. He twisted when he saw a foot headed toward his already abused nose. Groping along the bottom, he shuddered when he felt something soft and wet.

Someone needed a diaper change, he thought, *recognizing the familiar feel after changing thousands of them.*

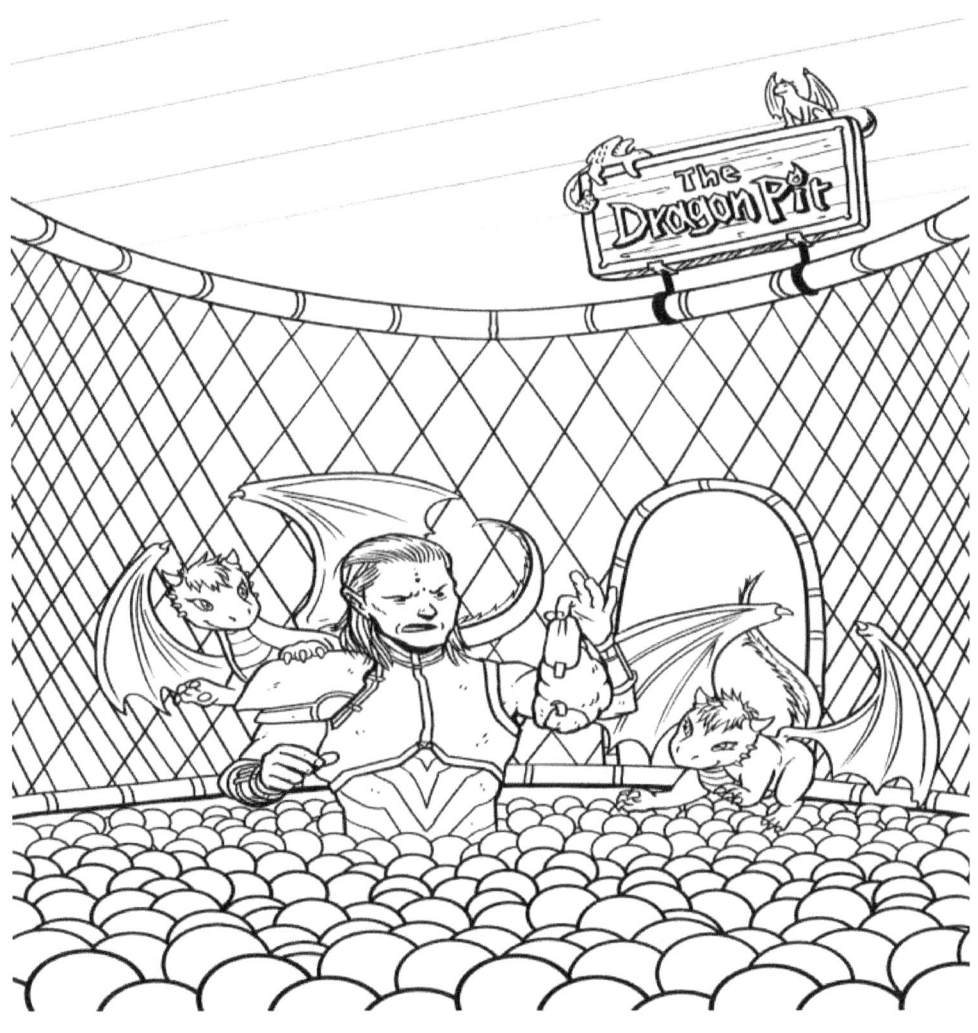

Popping up to draw in a deep breath of air, he quickly filled his lungs before sinking back down again. Pushing through the balls, he felt along the bottom. He was on his third pass, when he finally realized that with each one, he was finding fewer and fewer objects on the bottom. Surfacing for another breath, he saw that the crowd of observers had grown and that he was the center of their amusement.

"Lord Trelon, I believe this belongs to you?" The merchant said with a slightly disgruntled expression. "Weapons are not permitted in the ball pit."

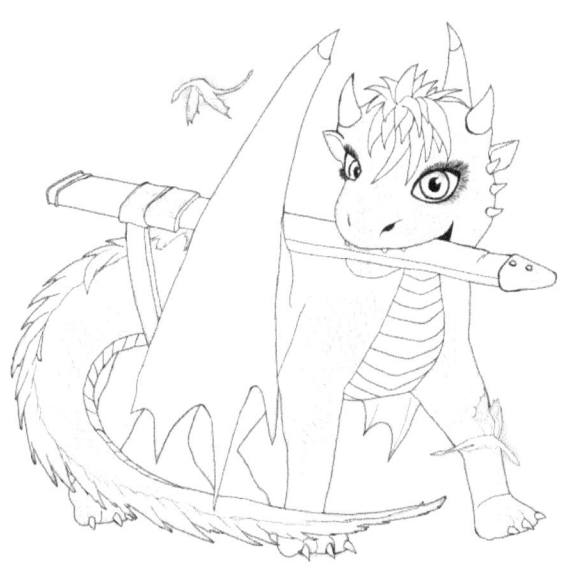

Trelon stood up, ignoring the snickers of the crowd. "Where did you find it?" He asked with a grimace, wading through the balls and hoping he didn't step on any submerged kids.

"Amber and Jade found it. They come daily to bring up the treasures lost among the balls," the merchant's wife said in delight.

"Daily?! But, where are they?" Trelon asked in astonishment, looking at the array of items lying on the table and labeled lost and found.

"They have gone to the candy shop," the merchant's wife said. "Down six rows and to the right. You had better catch them before they eat any. Lady Cara says the candy makes them more active."

"I don't see how that is possible," the merchant retorted under his breath, wincing when his wife slapped his arm.

"Six and to the right," Trelon muttered, climbing out of the ball pit and snatching up his knife. "Thank you."

"Good luck, Lord Trelon. I hope you catch them before they make it to the replicator repair shop! They like to put things in it," the merchant called after him.

Trelon pushed through the crowd. He was all too familiar with what Amber and Jade liked to do with the replicators! He was still finding demented symbiots in the house. He swore they were hiding them.

Hurrying down the street, he counted out the sixth row and turned right. His eyes widened in horror when he saw the huge candy store. It wasn't a small cart like many of the other merchants. It was a three story tall horror house of sugar. If Amber and Jade got lose inside it…. A shudder ran through him.

"This would be even worse than Cara on coffee," Trelon whispered, staring with wide, horrified eyes at the candy wheel.

Stumbling forward, Trelon was almost to the door when a familiar shape stepped out holding two tiny little girls in her arms. Trelon stopped and stared, his heart melting at the looks of love that passed between the trio before they turned to gaze at him with that same look.

"Did you lose something?" Cara asked with a soft, understanding smile.

"How did you know?" Trelon whispered, walking toward his beautiful mate.

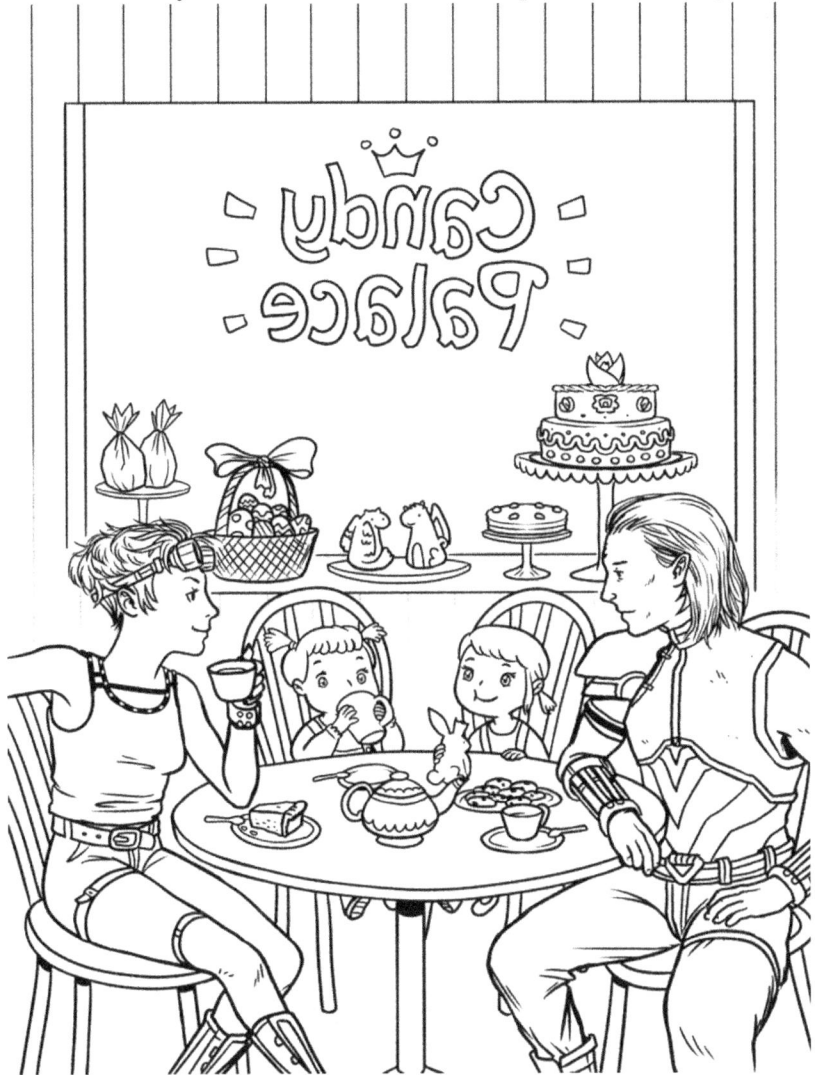

Cara chuckled and shook her head. "This is their favorite store. They love coming here," she replied. "I knew after watching you in the ball pit exactly where they would go next."

"Dada's, this for's you's," Amber said, holding out a lollipop the size of his palm.

"This's too's," Jade added with a grin. "I's onlys eats one bites."

Trelon laughed when he saw the missing ear of the chocolate rabbit. This was another sign of his wife's creativity. She had learned how to replicate chocolate and it had quickly become a favorite among their people.

"I wanted to surprise you with breakfast," he admitted, reaching for Jade.

Cara laughed and winked at him. "Well, I do know this great little place around the corner that serves coffee," she whispered, stepping close enough to brush a kiss against his lips. "They also have all different colors of hard boiled eggs," she added.

Eggs! Colored eggs! His dragon roared, perking up.

Now, you decide to wake up, Trelon growled in exasperation.

It time for breakfast, his dragon rumbled in delight.

"Breakfast it is," Trelon replied with a laugh, wrapping his free arm around Cara and Amber.

Draw your own adventure below.

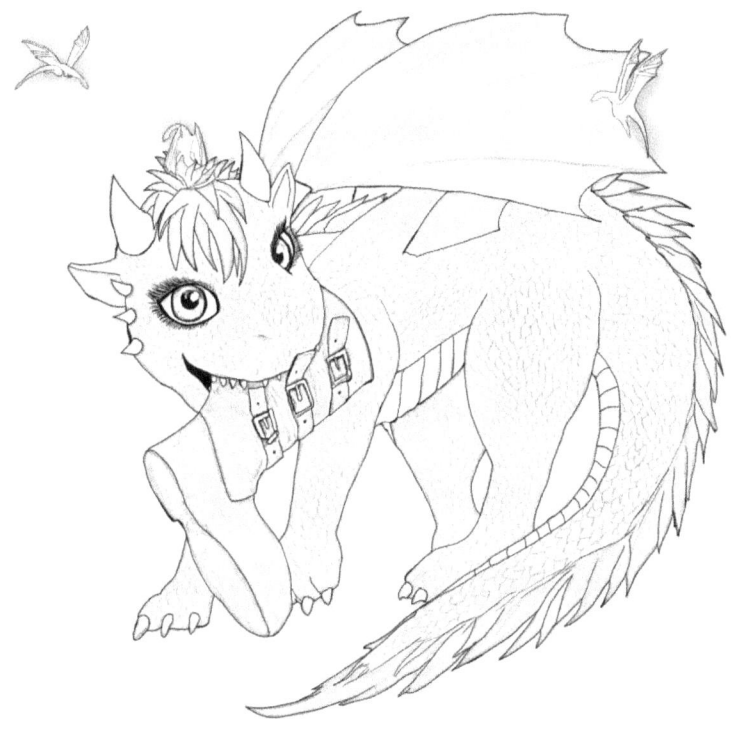

At the Market Scramble

TOW ☐☐☐ (11)

STSE ☐☐☐☐

DAKR ☐☐☐☐ (12)

DOGL ☐☐☐☐ (14)

EESY ☐☐☐☐

PEEDER ☐☐☐☐☐☐

RAPPISGADNIE ☐☐☐☐☐☐☐☐☐☐☐ (3)

TEANEBH ☐☐☐☐☐☐ (9)

FULORCOL ☐☐☐☐☐☐☐ (6)

LABLS ☐☐☐☐☐ (1)

KMEATR ☐☐☐☐☐☐ (13, 2)

SYOT ☐☐☐☐ (8)

FACE ☐☐☐☐ (4, 10)

LECOTHOAC ☐☐☐☐☐☐☐☐☐ (7)

BARSEKTAF ☐☐☐☐☐☐☐☐☐ (5)

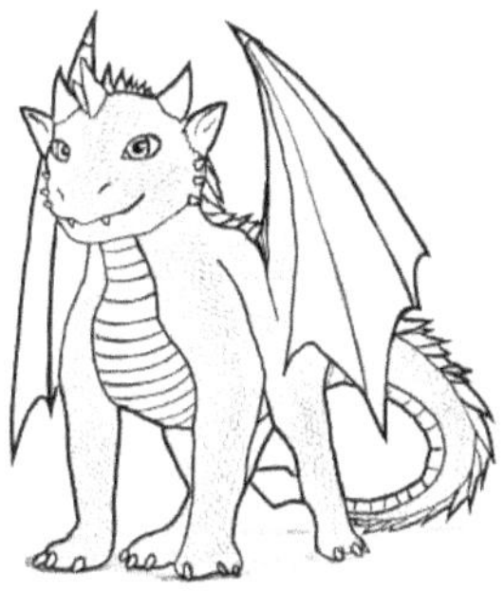

☐☐☐☐☐☐☐☐☐ ☐☐☐ ☐☐☐
1 2 3 4 5 6 7 8 9   10 11 12   13 14 13

Place words for each number below to find the word.

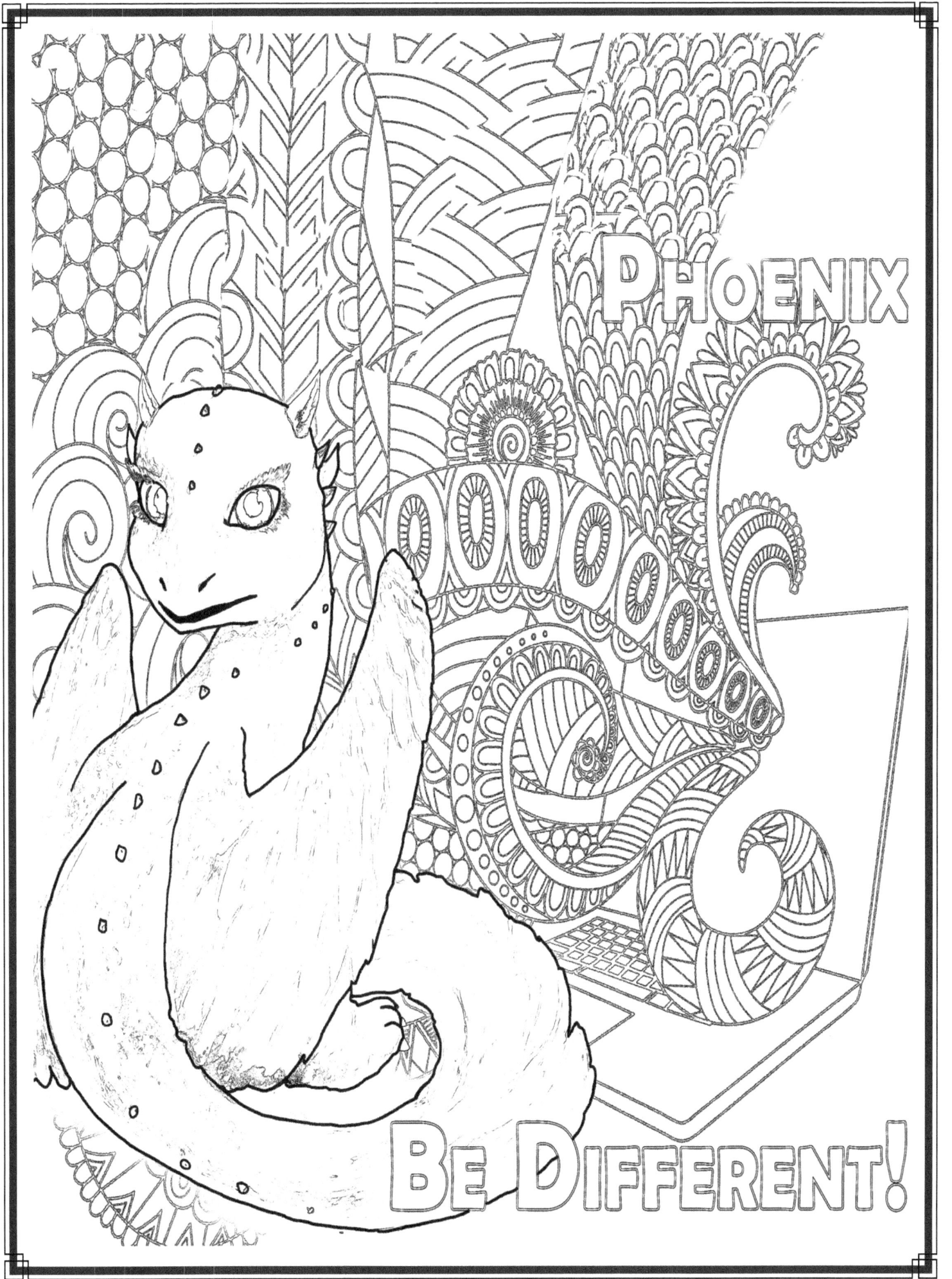

Dragon's Pit

```
G Z W R Q J P F F N A P C Y O Q O J K J V E F Z H
E N D P L Z F D Z I O D Y P J S K O O B F G J L W
R H I B X D P O L T N S L O U X D B X I G I W N G
Z C J H H G K G Q O S E U W Z Z R N N J C P Z M P
B B X H C A H G L G N Y M E W S Y K T U F S R O U
T T W L Q R W P J R P F K D Q Y X V R E M T V R Y
C A F E V K A R X L C O L O R E D E N M C V E Z T
T B Q X C W C E J V Q F Z N A L P R Z U D T X T E
H L T H E M B N S L V S A O M A M R E F R S I W H
D E T S I W T R E L O N H S I T E J B B I P P G A
N U C H B R D Z M O V M W D T D T K A Y L B R I T
G B U M A G T Y U S S Q A X S R A L X L L U T X Q
D F F R N X T N S T F P C Y X P L W A Q N F P J U
V S H I M C I Z D C Q S O F J S O B O T D N R A X
B W N R F F J M R S O B B E Y W C D E J D J T I O
K E X P E D A J A G W L E B L B O D N T D A Y K P
Q I Y B E G R K G N S E R J F B H A K U R T D F S
R H J I F P J O O T L S X I R Q C M J N O B E S P
R E B F F I Z Y N N R F C E N N C I A I K F L A U
Y S I P O N K L L I W A A Z F G S W W R A E I R S
F Z R D C N O Y I W R K Y K J J O O H L K V G E H
O E O Q L U O I N A F S R E T H G U A D L E H B E
C S V M S A W V G A Q E A R C V E G S G H A T M D
H E A R E N V K S Q F S V F Y K L Q W A O R E A E
I E P Q Z B N T H Z Q M Q L X S A D J B B F Y C Y
```

AMBER
BALLPIT
BALLS
BOOKS
BREAKFAST
CAFE
CARA
CHOCOLATE
COFFEE
COLORED
COLRING
DAUGHTERS
DELIGHT
DIAPER
DRAGONLINGS
FAST
FOUND
GRUNTED
JADE
KNIFE
LOST
MARKET
PUSHED
RUN
SEARCHING
TRELON
TWISTED
VALDIER

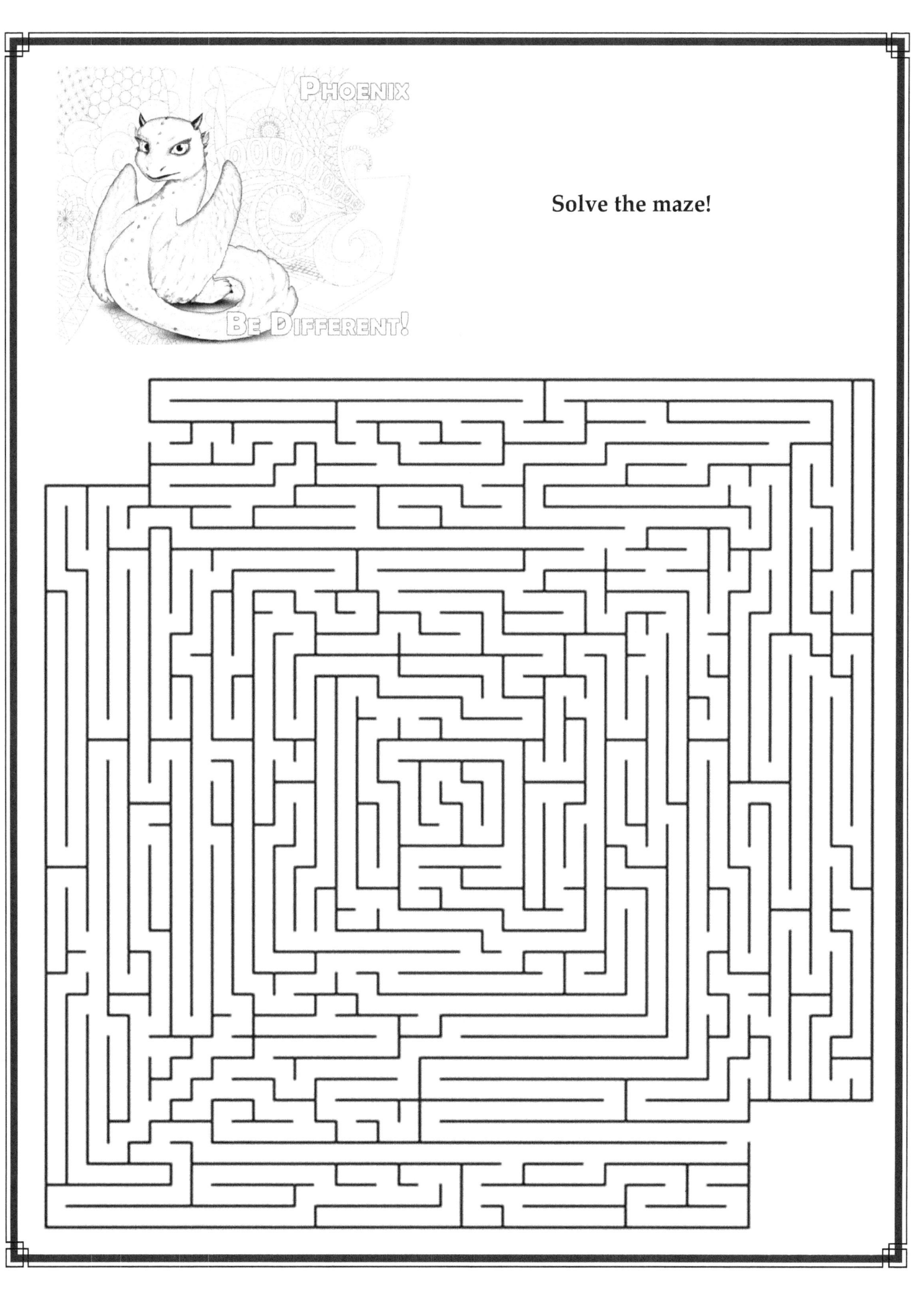

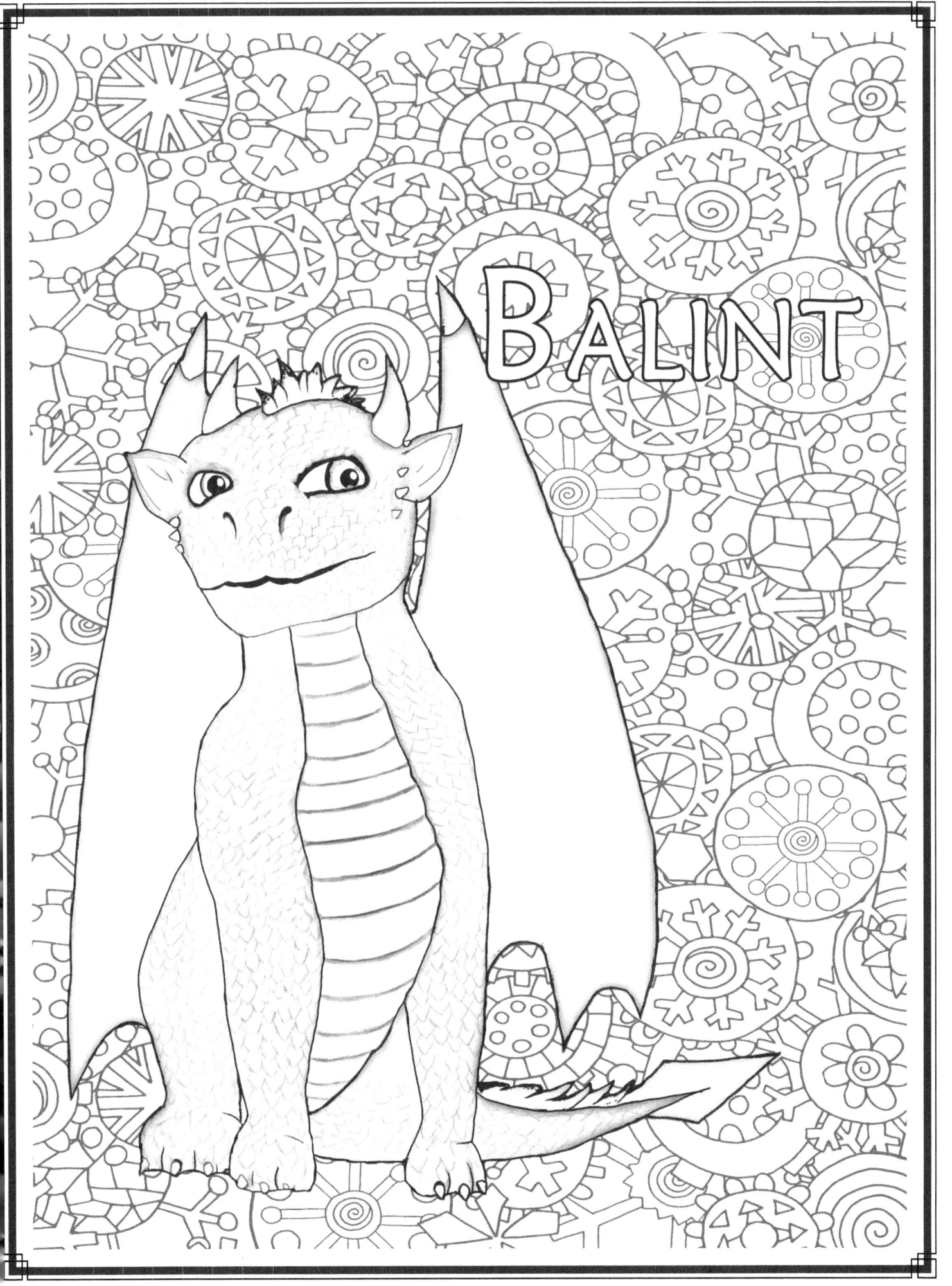

Hidden Phrase: Dragonlings of Valdier

Hint: Phrase can be found in the story above.

A	B	C	D	E	F	G	H	I	J	K	L	M	N	O	P	Q	R	S	T	U	V	W	X	Y	Z
P																								B	

_ _   _ A _ _ _ _   _ _ _ A _   _ _ _ _   _ _ _ _ Y _ _
I N   J P G M I N Q   P E   G I N   G O A B   U S Z Q N A

_ _ _ A _ _   _ _ _ _   _ _ _   _ _ _ _ _ _   _ _ _
Q V P U S A E   G S S R   S W W   G I V S T U I   G I N

_ _ _ _ .
M V S J Q

Draw your own adventure with Balint, Alice and Jabir below.

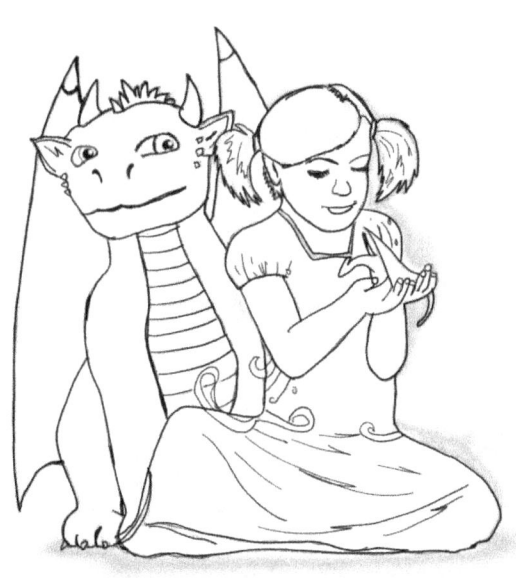
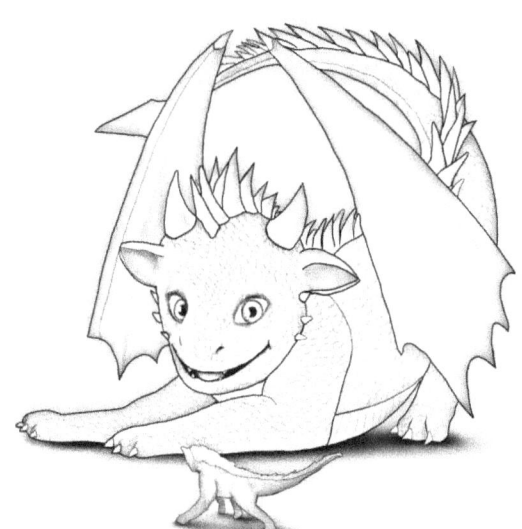

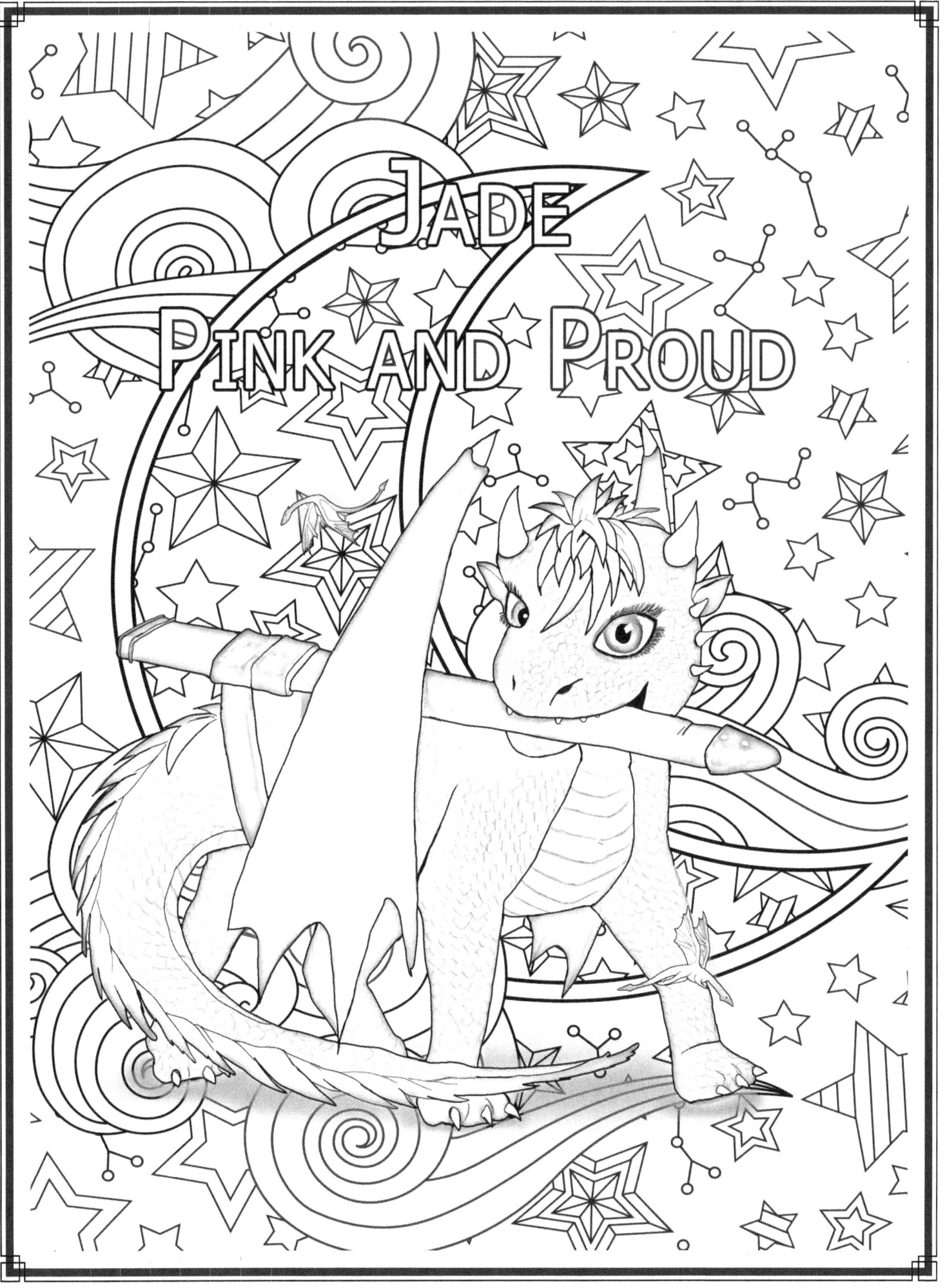

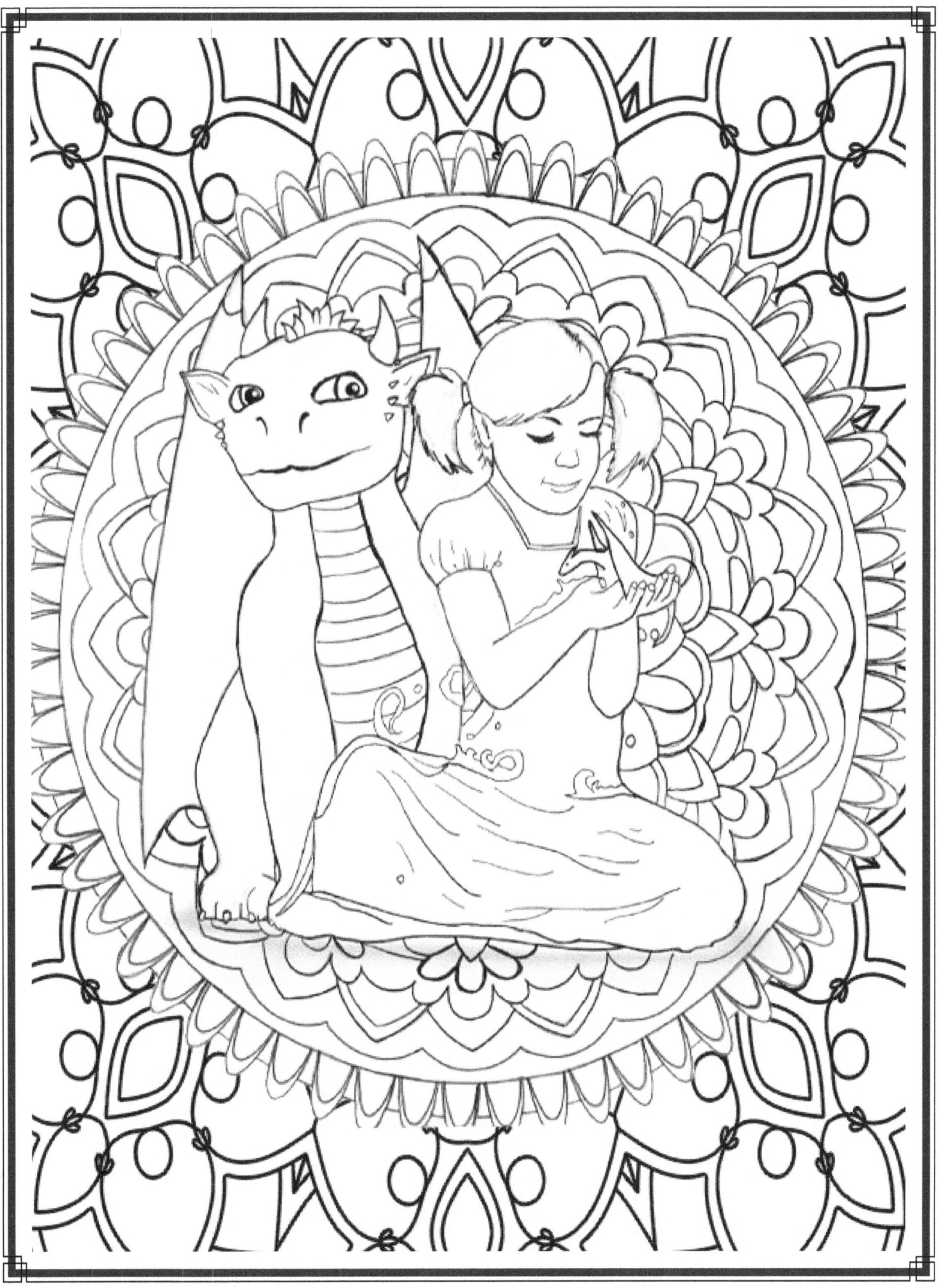

Word Search: Dragonlings of Valdier

```
R Y O M S Q G W W T N J I X X E G F W R J W N L V
E F W M U X B N Y S C X G Q N O I I U A I A V A N
I D M Q O M C F I L V N S P A C E G D G L B L S H
D O M Q I T E K P N I B F Y K N J E C I D E A V O
L F Q R C D S W A T N M G S H X Y P C Y N S Z J P
A U A U E C O M F J S U A B Y D R E W T O E G H E
V A A Q R Z O I D O X U R F L M S E I O I T R H X
D S G I P E H B C U V E D X K U B N T N B A L E O
K M F D K S O H A R S G U E A Q E A P H C M N M G
U V Y C S A P Z C N P U Q M K S X N M P G W A W W
R E B M A U T I F E R A D V E N T U R E S U N H Y
S Q T K L L O E L Y I B Y L I E C Y W J B U A E B
A L I E N S R K R X N M A P X I N E O H P O V L A
S A M T S I R H C I G O A B H Z K I C V F R E P L
D A S V O Z T J E O N R V O I U E D W C A L P S I
O F S Y M B I O T S E A D N R E Z L W H I I W K N
C R M H Q J W T U N M A C R I J S O I M H N G G T
Y I A C U D G G T I N E V O L X E G S S E R W O H
W E G X U V M S K G J D X K C B X P R K G P T V F
Y N D O R A R R E T S A E Q E S F A L K Z E L A L
E D U P D F L R H G C N D R C F W L A A S T Z C O
B S P T G D G O M I J I I U J J A L O O N J X Y M
X H Q Y E V E E R C Z X X J N S U D E C O E H O P
M I N Z F G L S Y L J Z X D A G H U M A N S T Y Y
Z P H C X B L Q S F K U U K J U N M O E U S A I V
```

Find the words below:

ADVENTURES
AIKATERINA
ALICE
ALIENS
AMBER
BABIES
BALINT
BIO
CHRISTMAS
DANGER
EASTER
FAMILY
FRIENDSHIP
GODDESS
GOLDIE
HARVEY
HOPE
HUMANS
JABIR
JADE
JOURNEY
LAUGHTER
LOVE
MATES
PARENTS
PHOENIX
PLANET
PRECIOUS
ROAM
RUNNING
SHIFTING
SMILE
SPACE
SPRING
SYMBA
SYMBIOTS
VALDIER
VALENTINES
WARSHIP

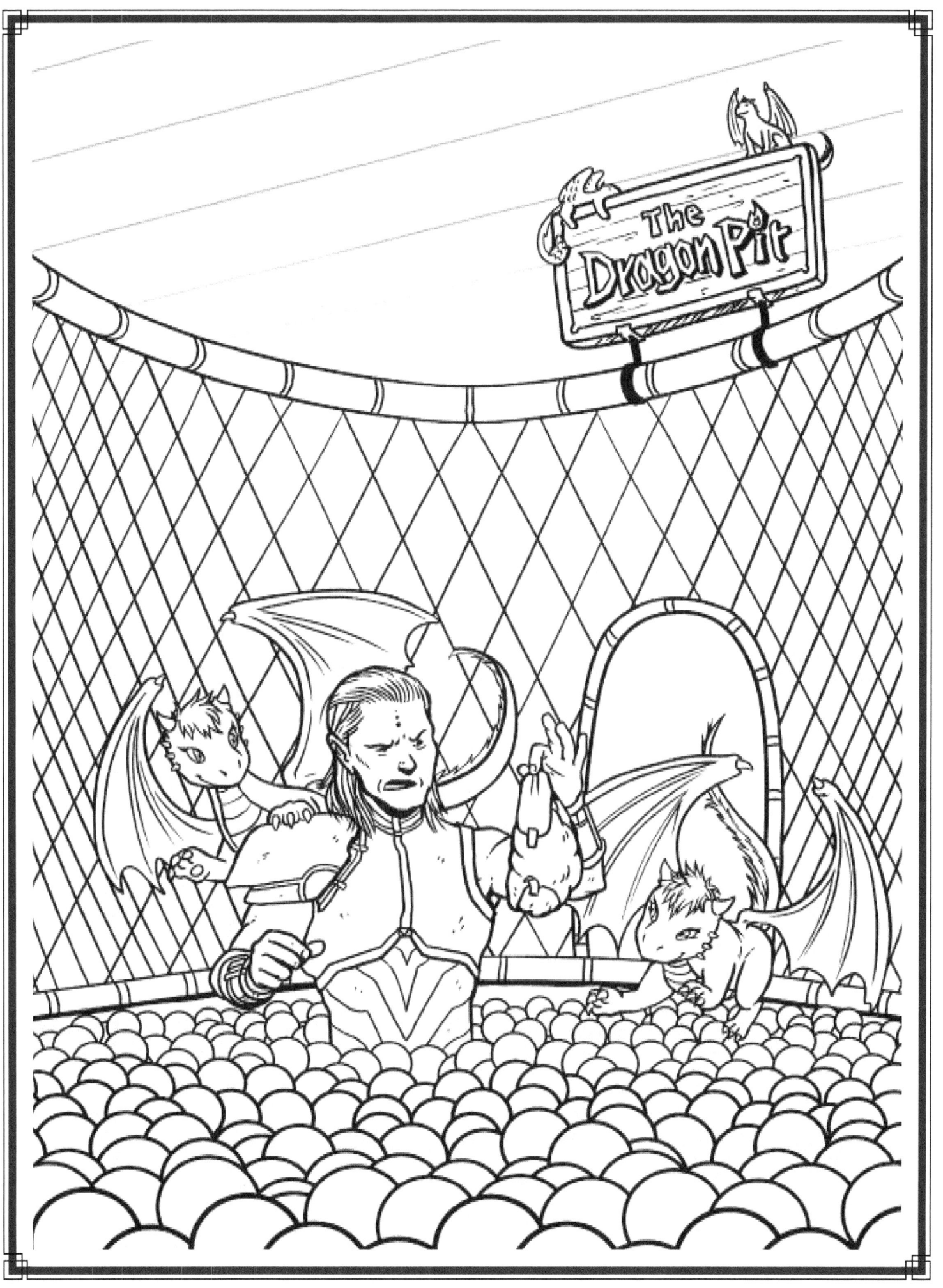

Solve the Maze

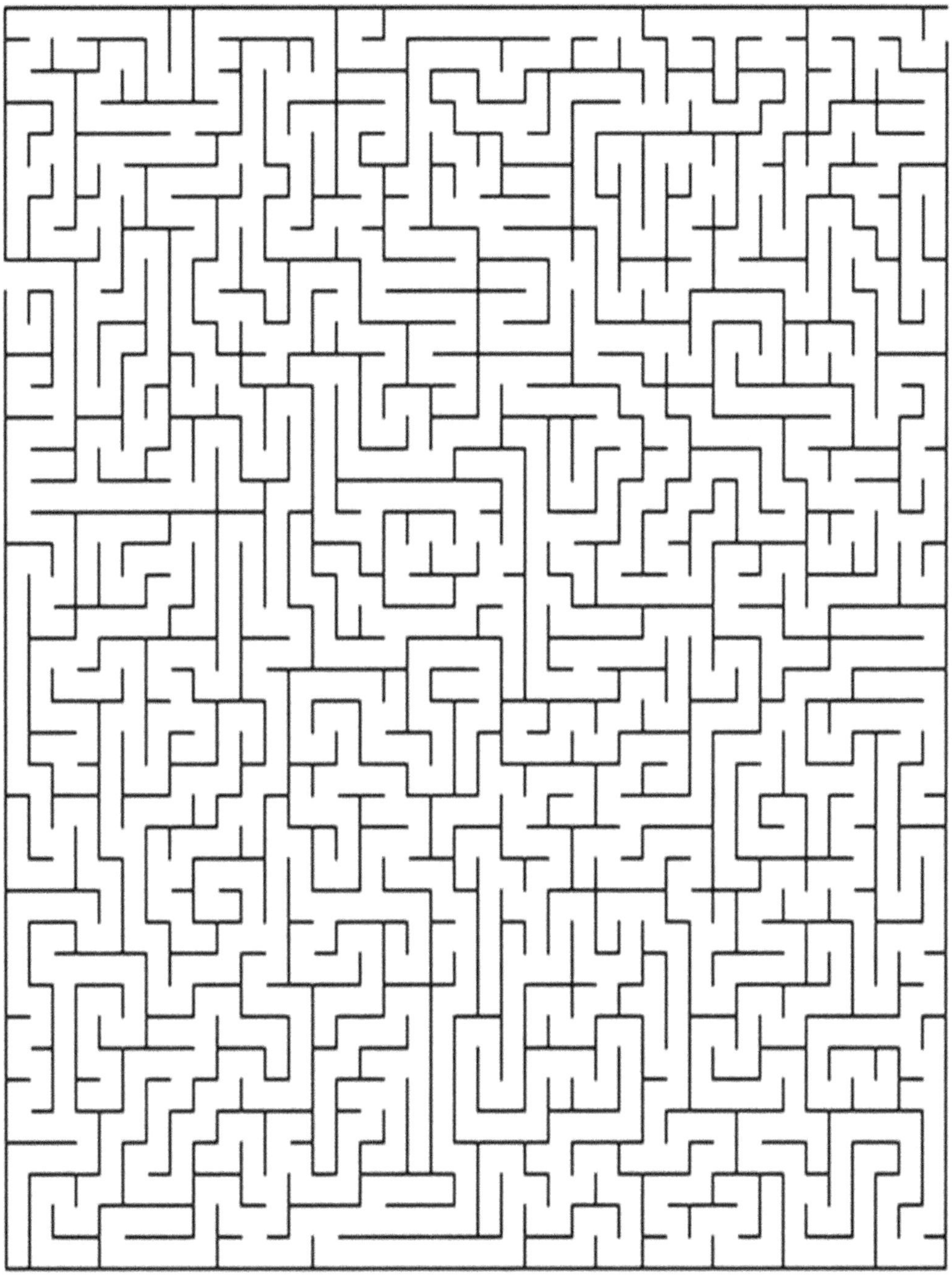

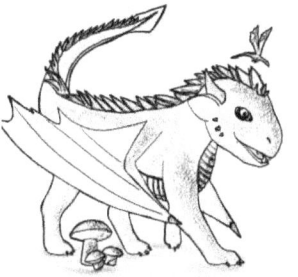

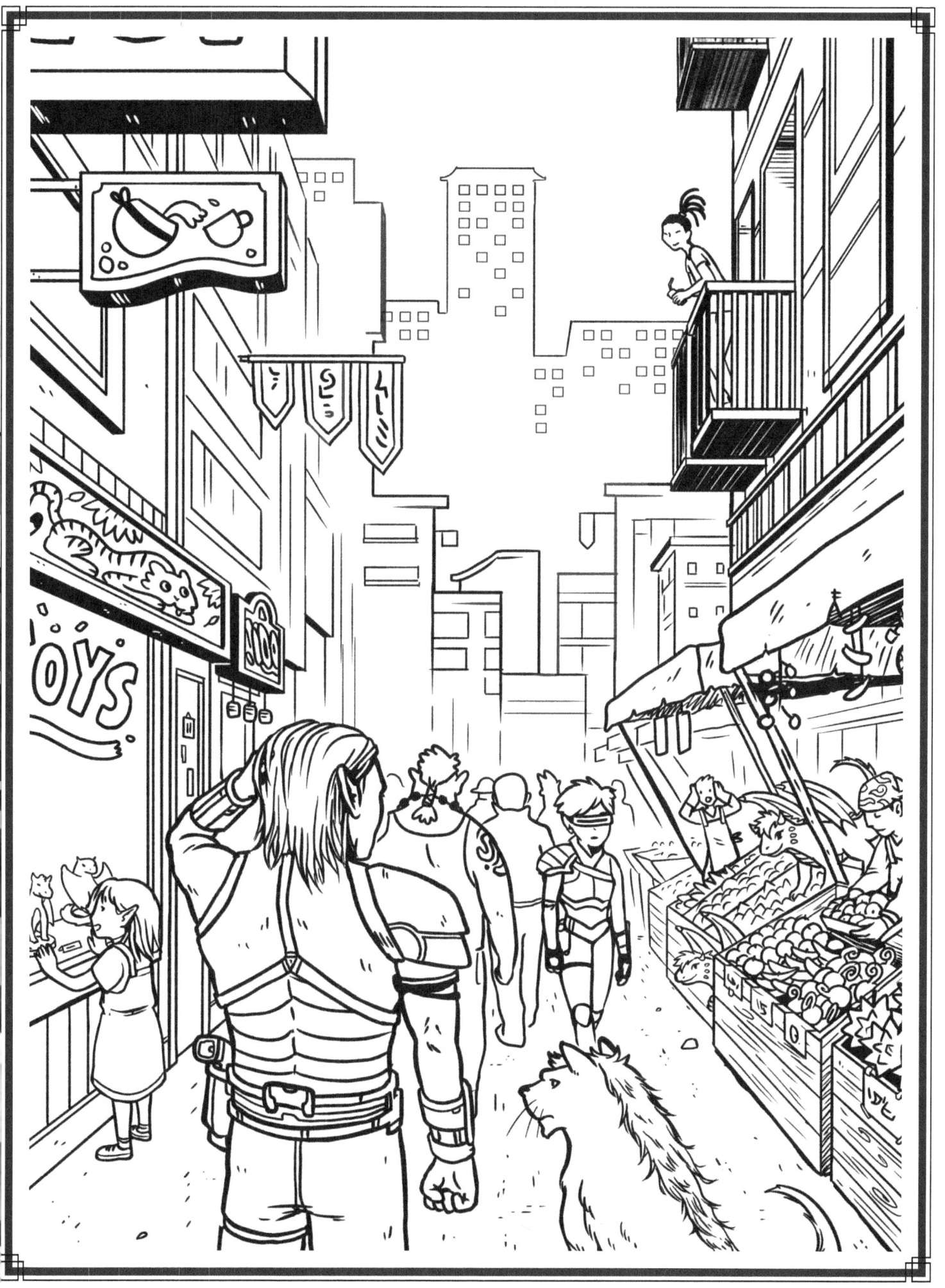

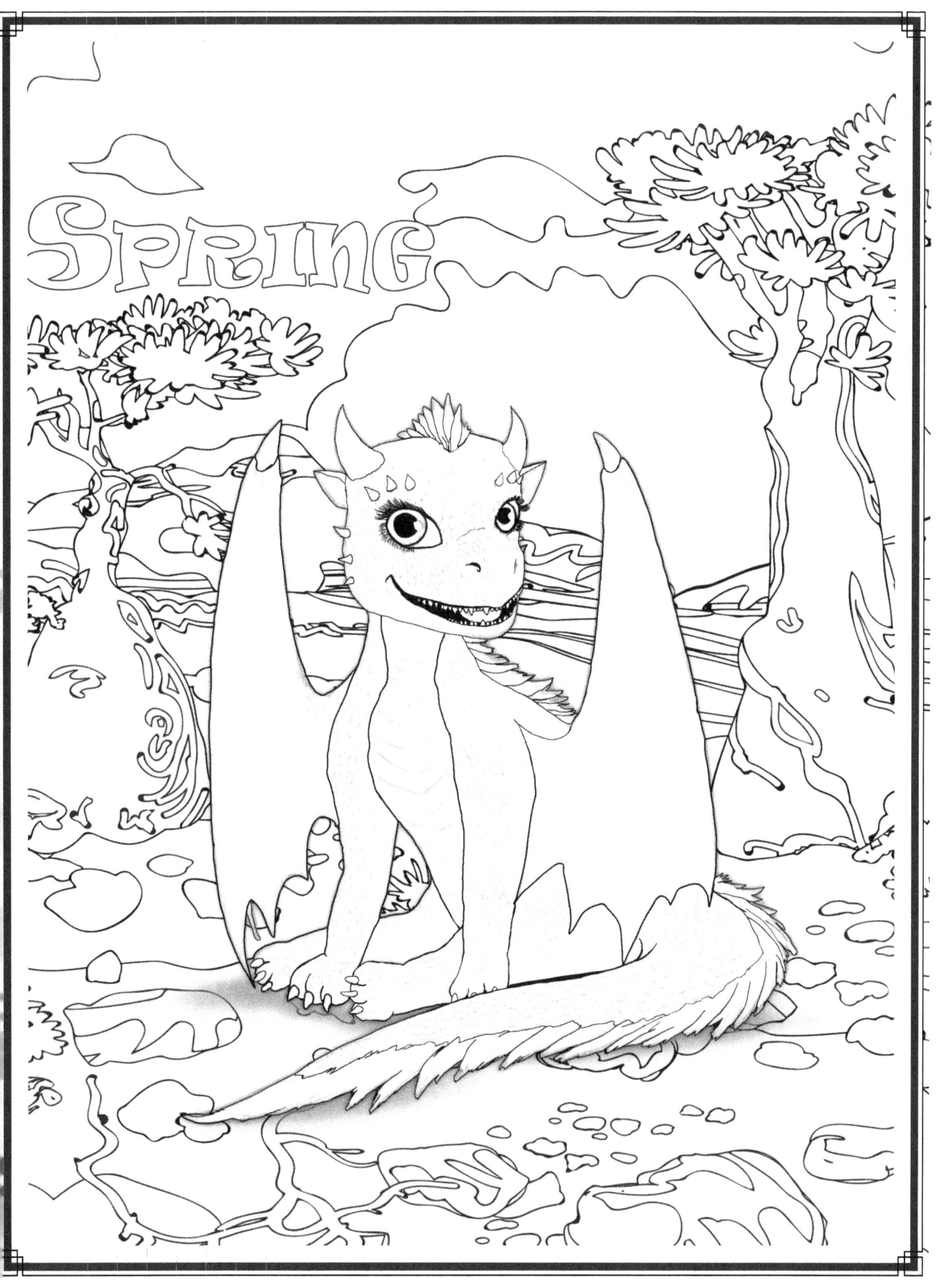

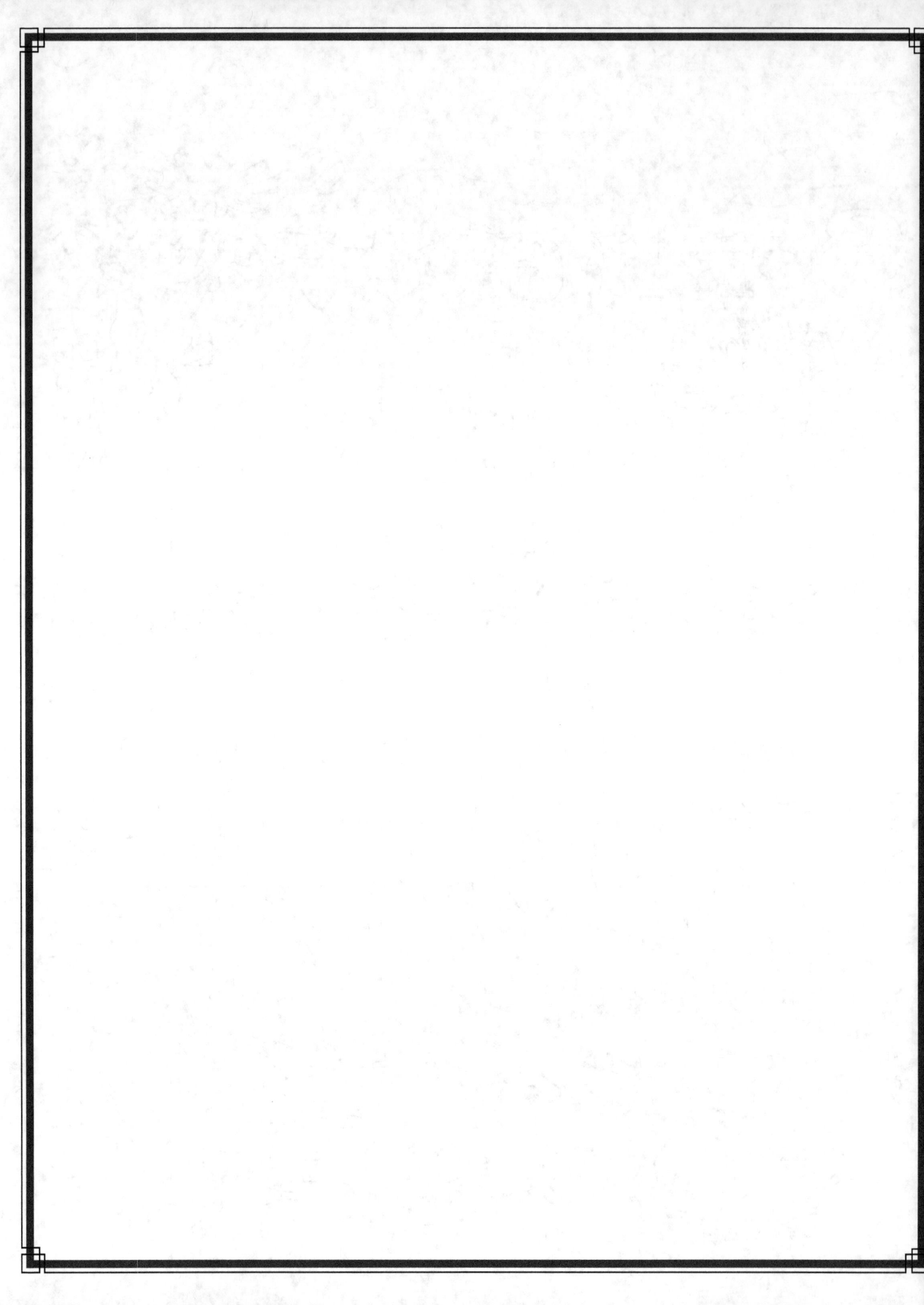

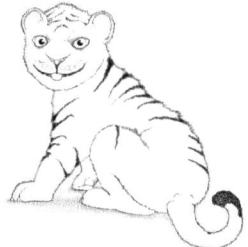

Create a Diamante Poem!

_____
Topic—a noun

_____ _____
Adjective adjective

_____ _____ _____
Verb verb verb

_____
Four-word phrase

_____ _____ _____
Verb verb verb

_____ _____
Adjective adjective

_____
Renaming noun

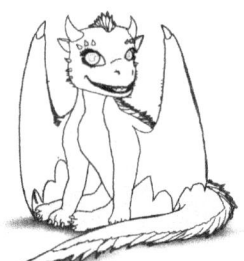

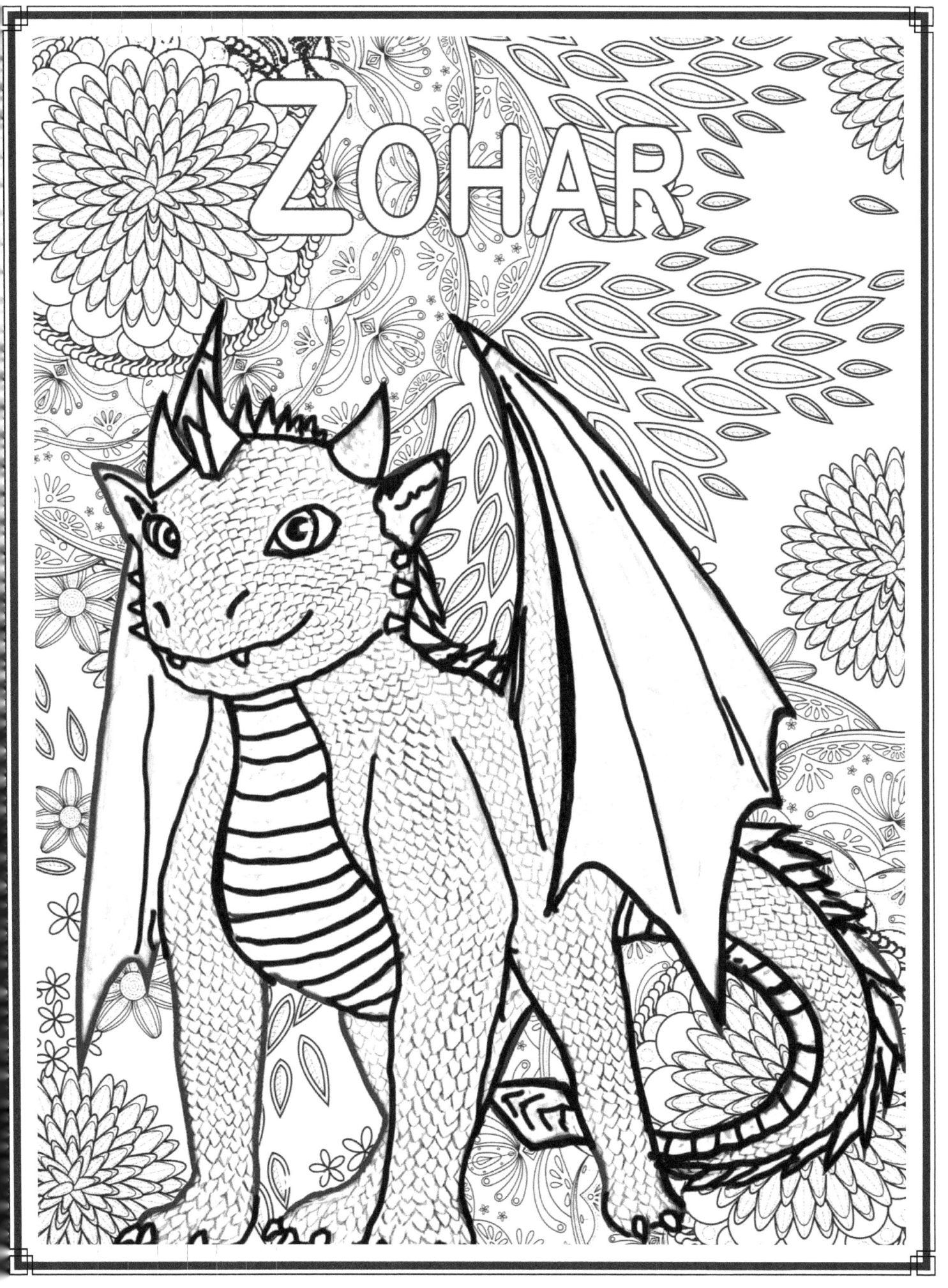

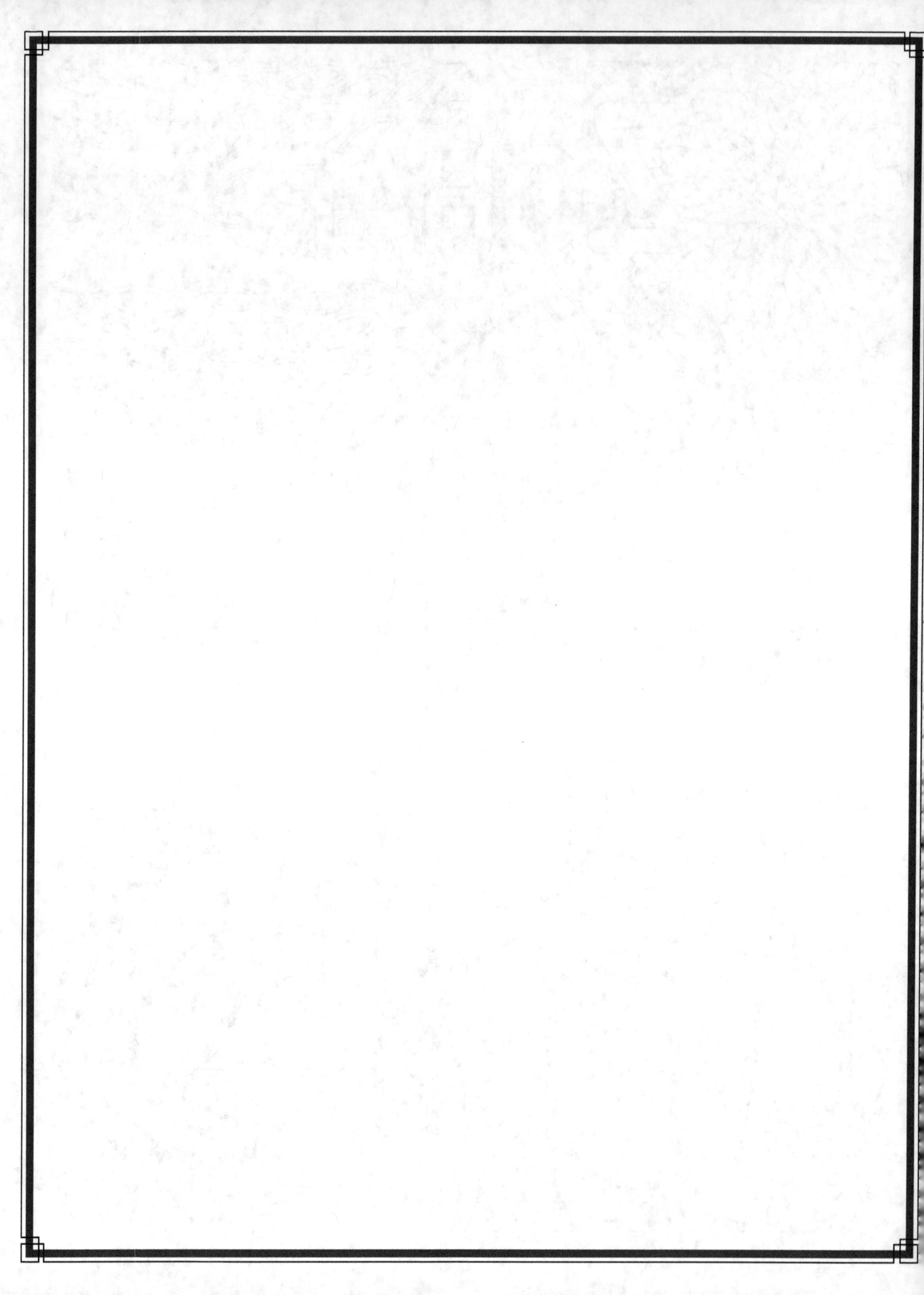

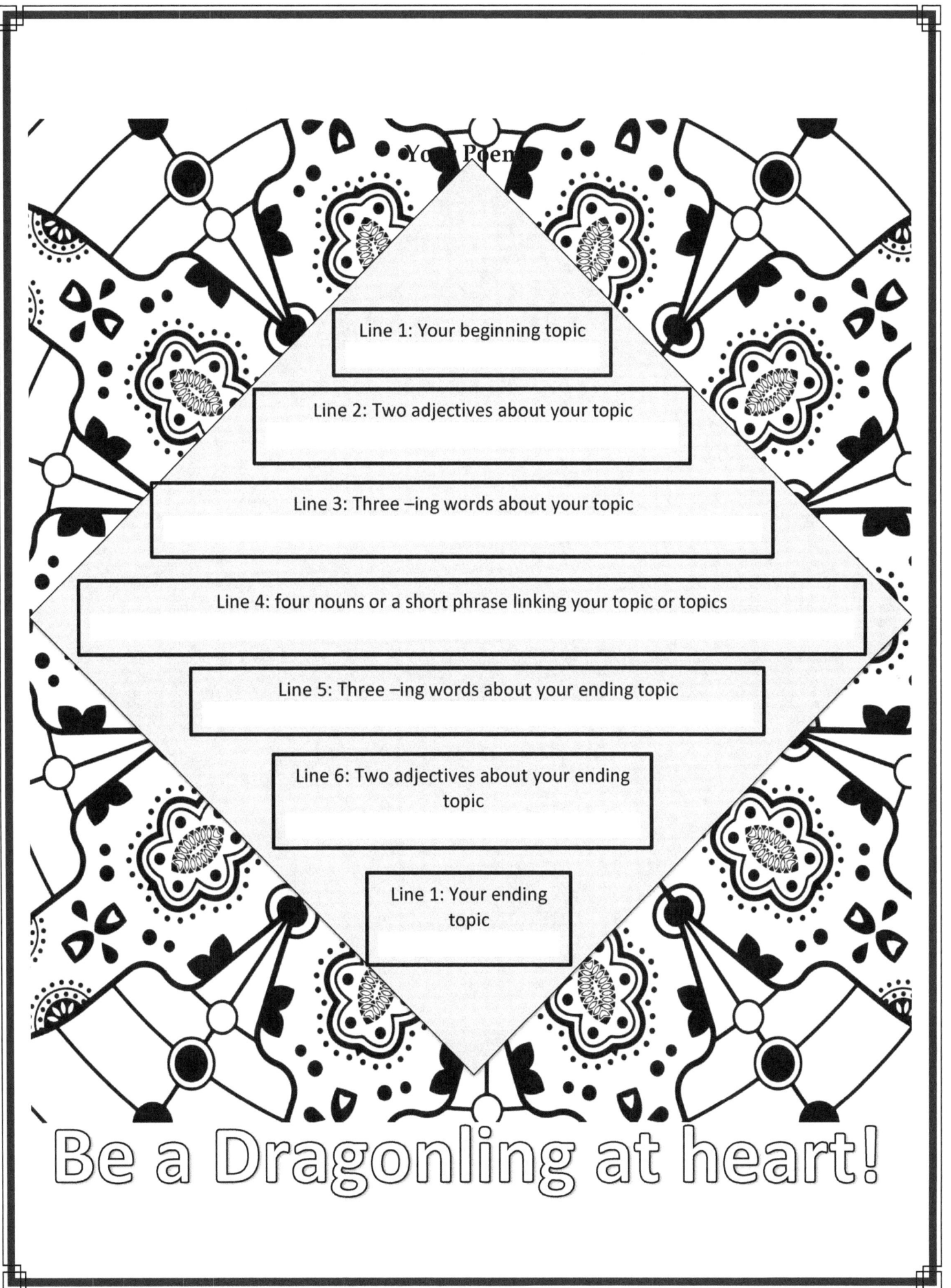

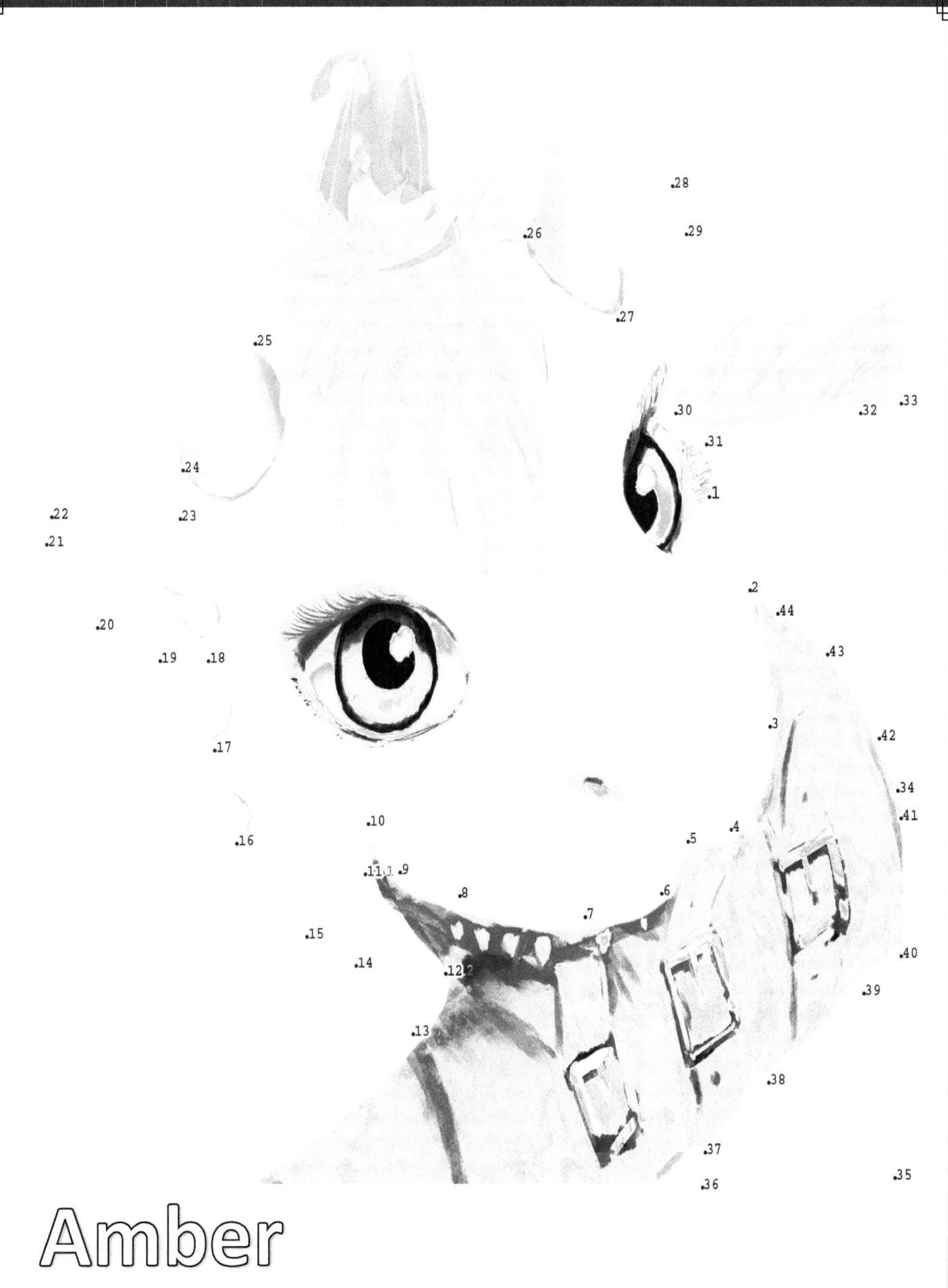

Amber

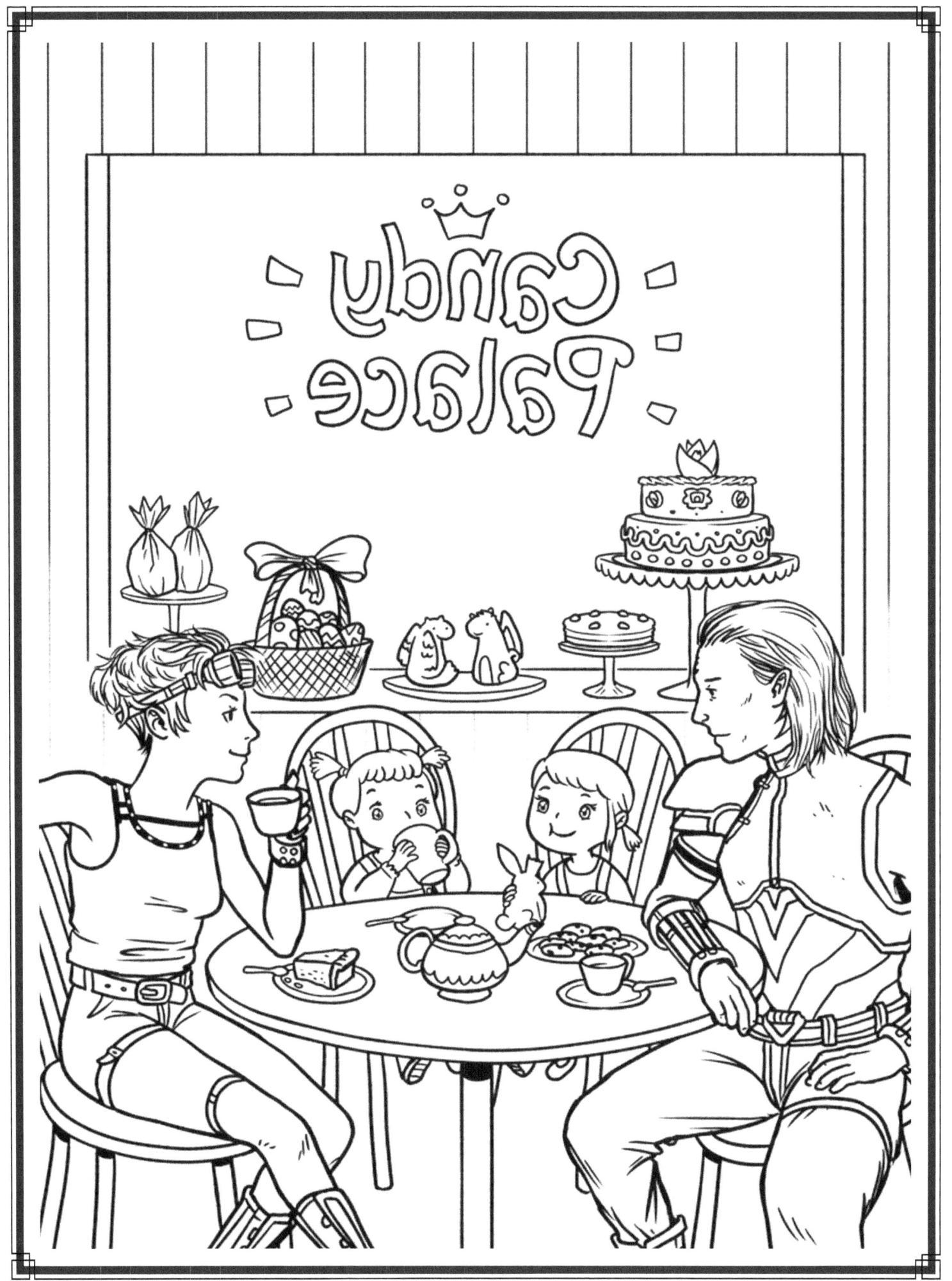

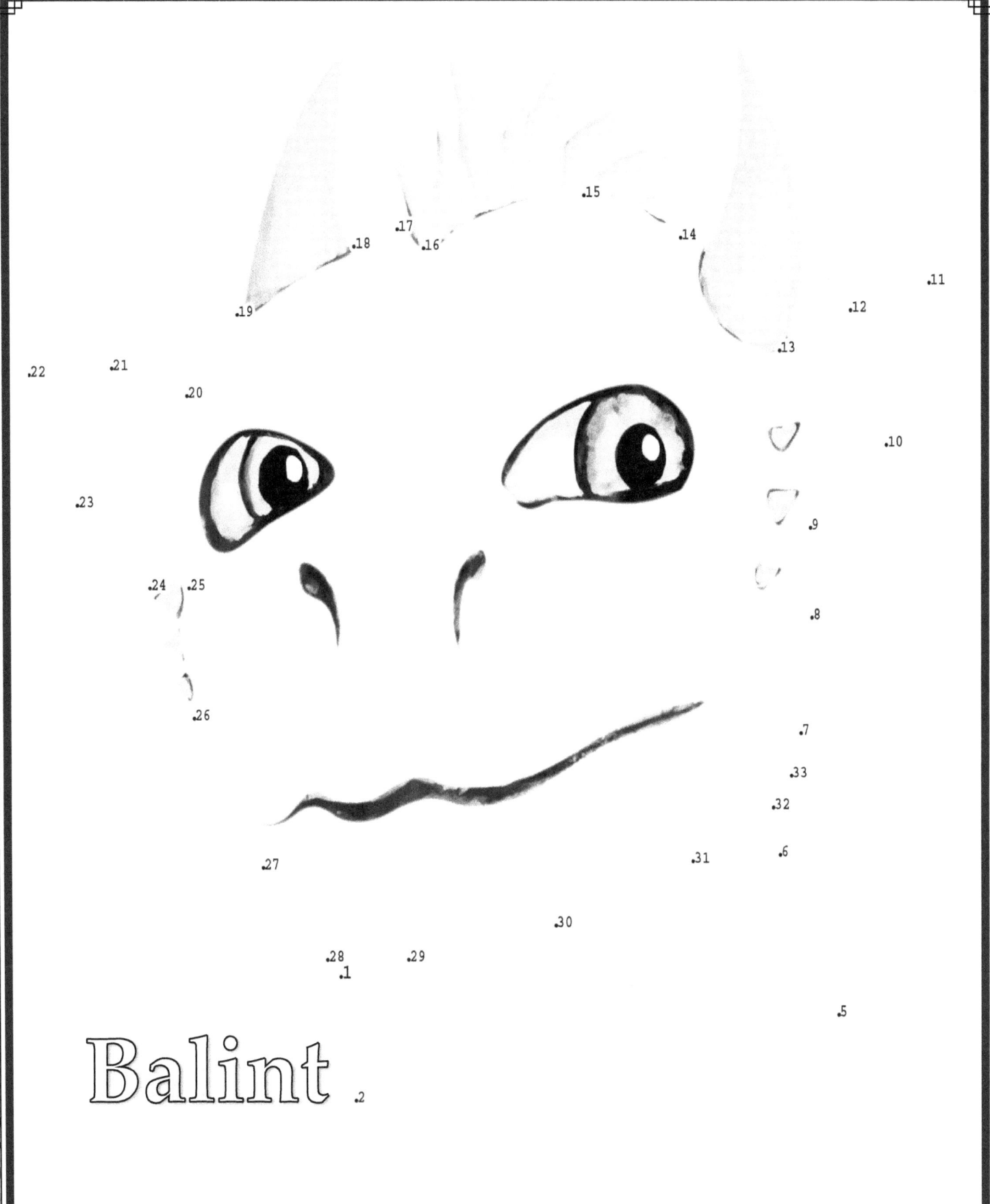

Draw your own picture with the emus from The Great Easter Bunny Hunt!

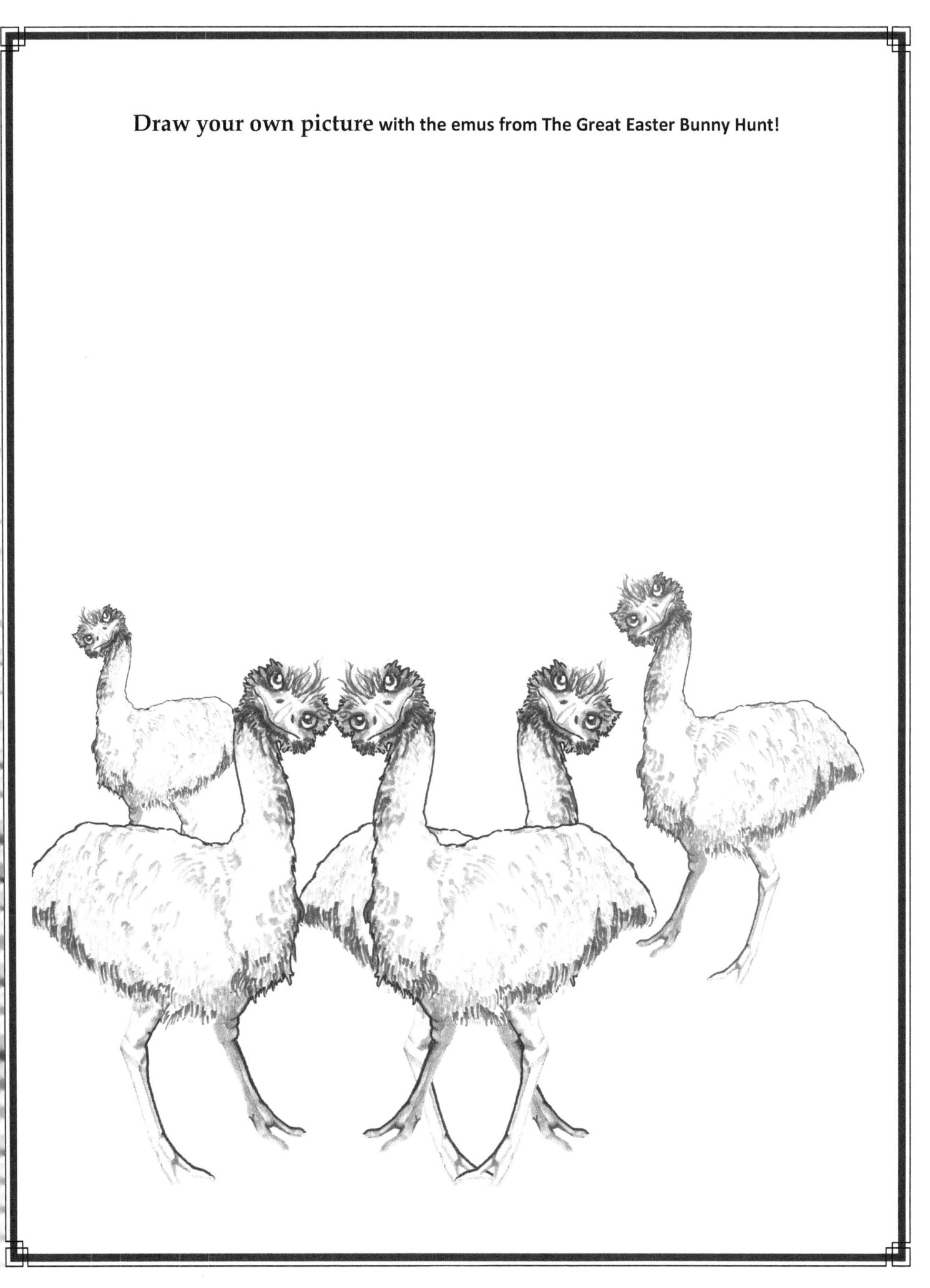

Unscramble each of the clue words.
Copy the letters in the numbered cells to other cells with the same number

VOLE — ☐☐☐☐

TUNDEERVA — ☐☐₁☐☐☐☐☐☐☐

DNSOARG — ☐☐☐☐☐☐₉☐

PALTESN — ☐☐☐☐☐☐☐

RASLO MESSYT — ☐☐☐☐☐☐ ☐☐₁₁☐☐☐☐☐

GAXYAL — ☐₁₀☐☐☐☐☐

TARSS — ☐☐☐☐☐

NIRSEVUE — ☐☐₆☐☐☐☐☐☐

SEIANL — ☐☐☐₈☐☐☐

DILNARSOGGN — ☐☐☐₃☐☐☐☐☐☐☐

TEASM — ☐☐☐☐☐

PETSARN — ☐☐☐☐☐☐☐

FIMYAL — ☐☐☐☐☐☐

HILADSYO — ☐☐☐☐☐☐☐☐

REITOSS — ☐☐☐☐☐☐☐

NONMITSAU — ☐☐☐☐☐☐☐☐☐

VSRIRE — ☐☐☐☐☐☐

SOSBYMTI — ☐☐☐☐☐☐☐☐

JAED — ☐☐☐☐

MABRE — ☐☐☐☐☐

RAMO — ☐☐☐☐

RAOHZ — ☐☐☐☐₂☐

NILTAB — ☐☐☐₇☐☐☐

RAJBI — ☐☐☐☐☐

NOEHIXP — ☐☐☐☐₅☐☐☐

PIRGSN — ☐☐☐☐☐₄☐

CAELI — ☐☐☐☐☐

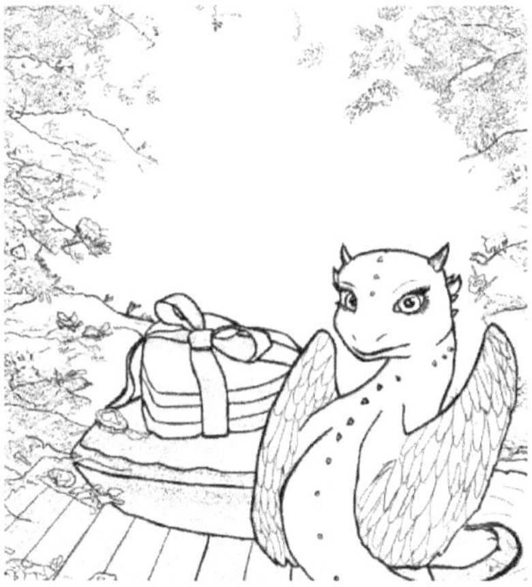

☐₁☐₂☐₃☐₄☐₅☐₆☐₇☐₈☐₉☐₁₀☐₁₁

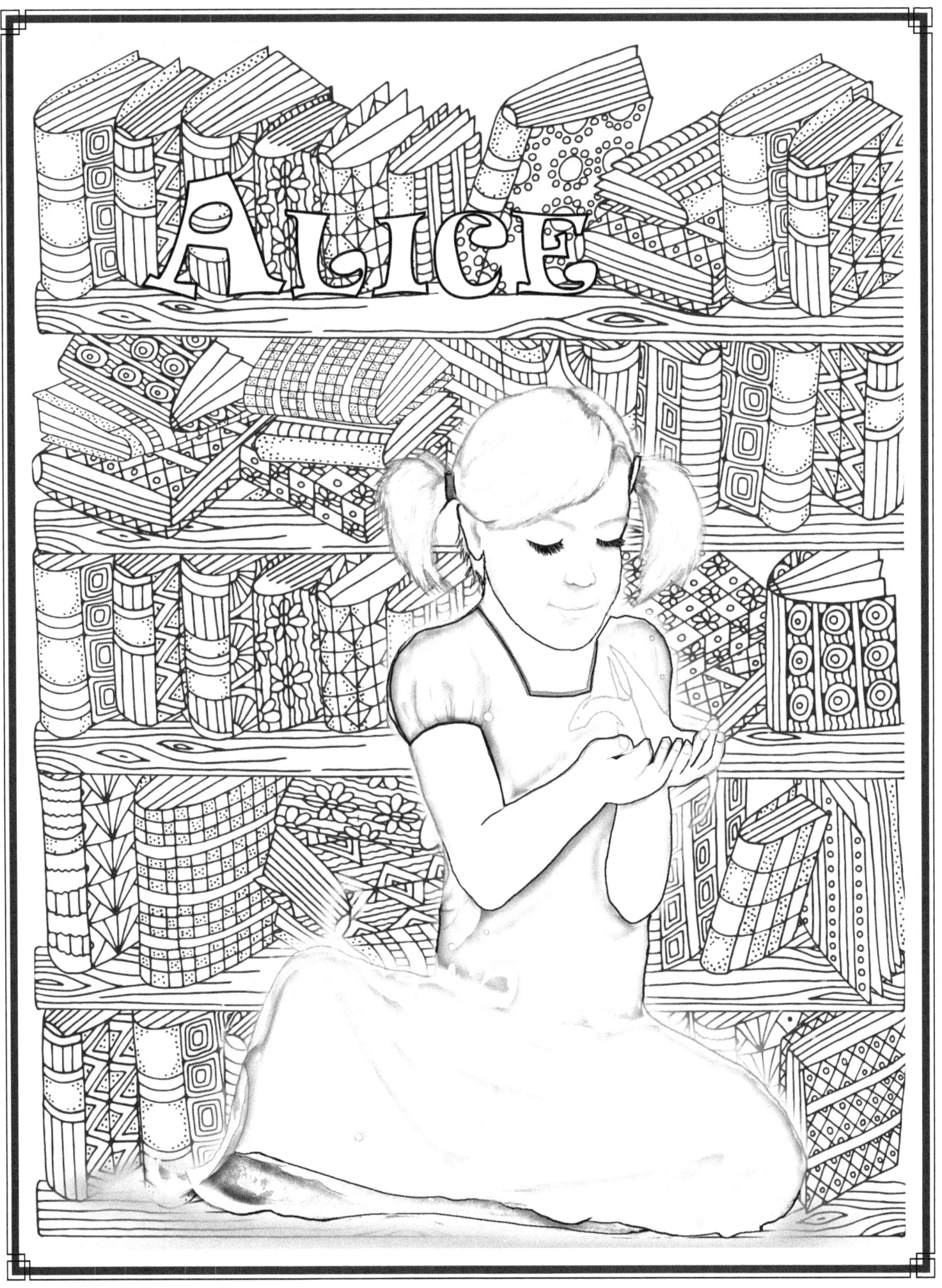

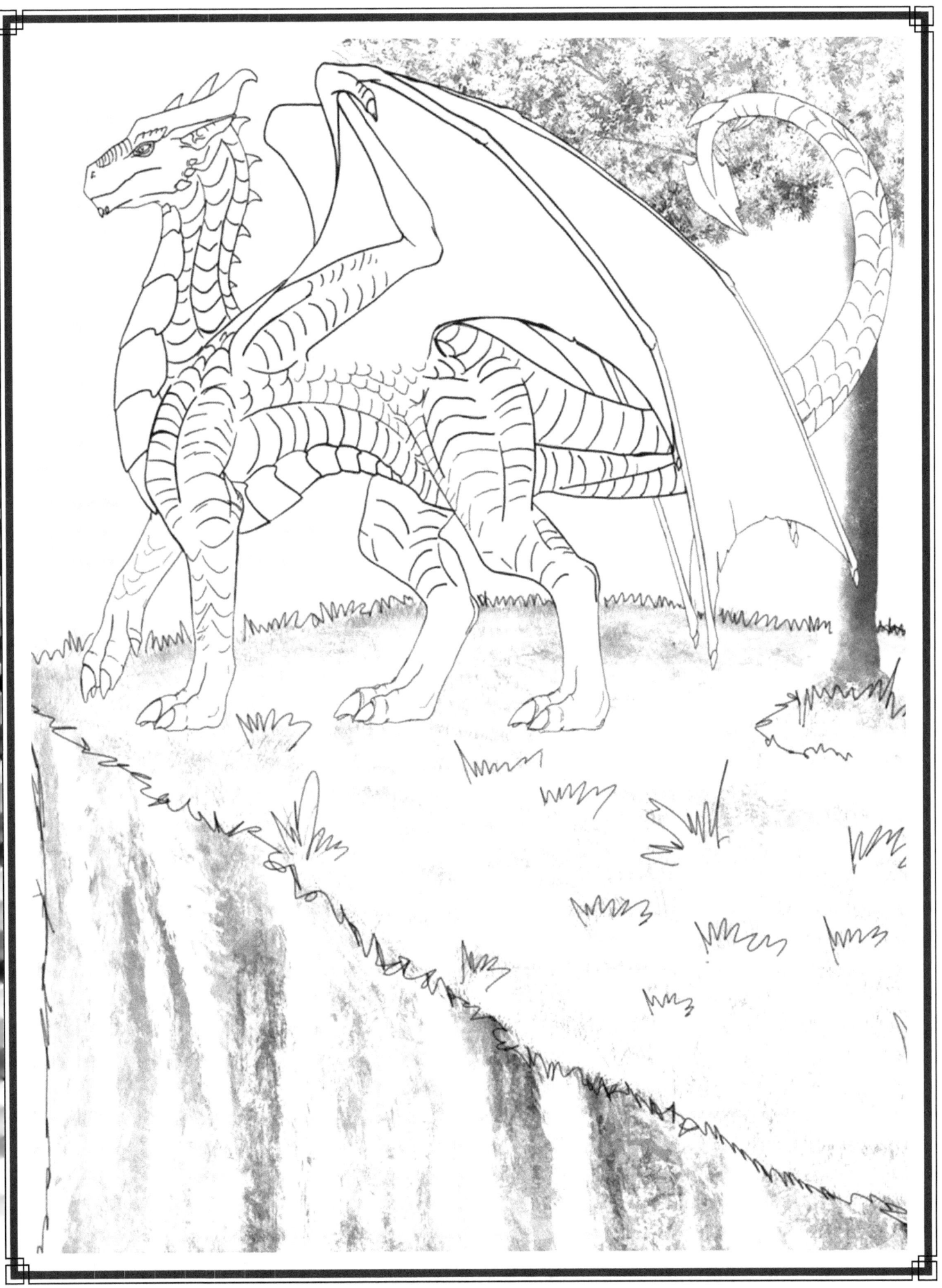

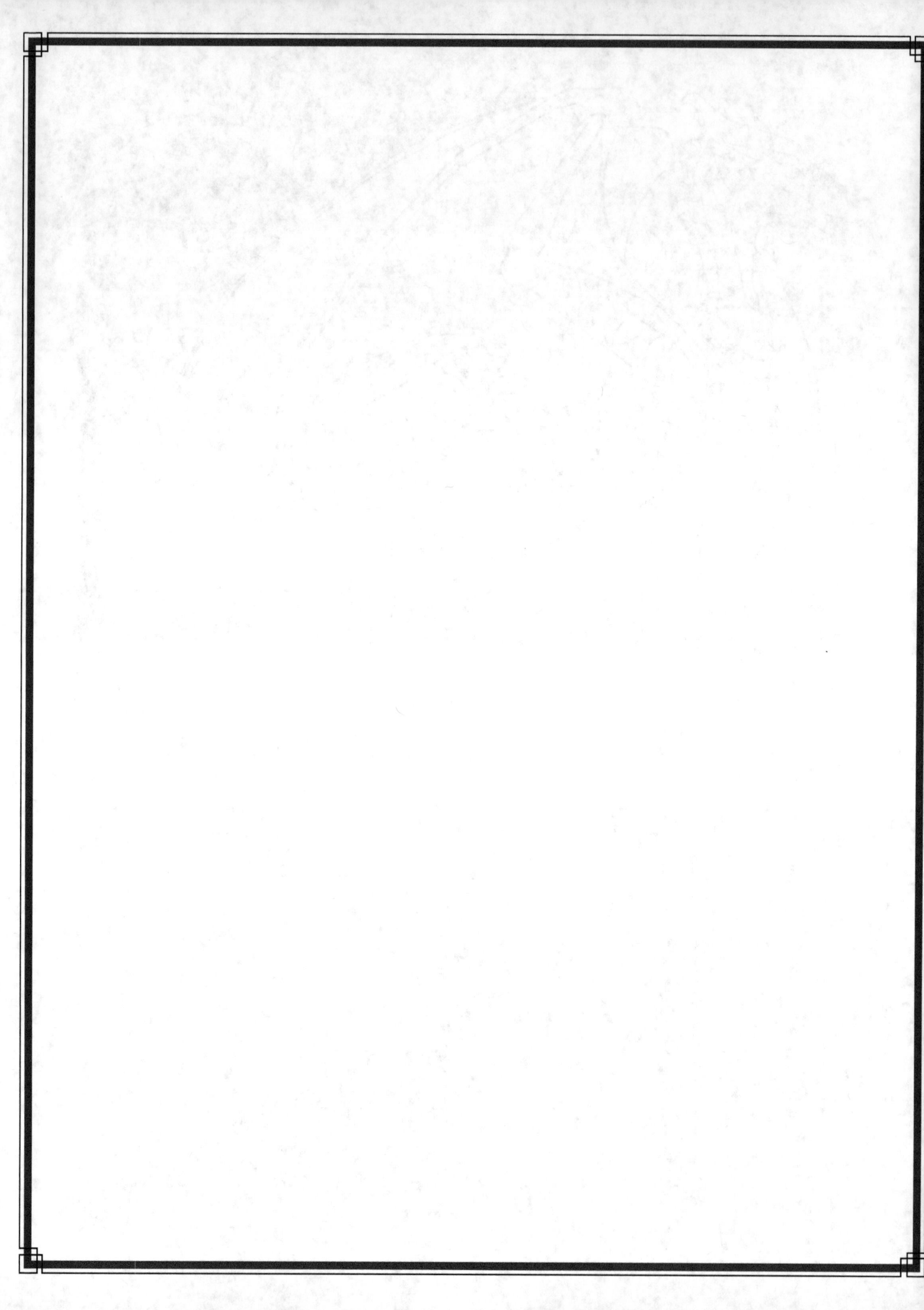

Missing Numbers

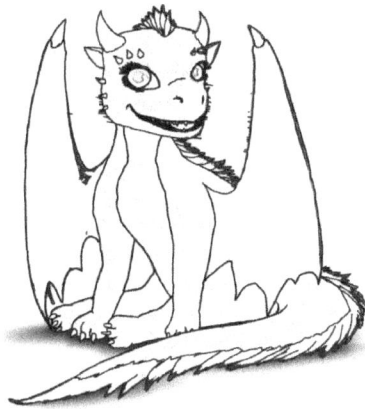

	-		+		11
+	■	+	■	×	
	×		-		2
+	■	+	■	+	
	-		×		-23
10		12		62	

Try to fill in the missing numbers.

Use the numbers 1 through 9 to complete the equations.

Each number is only used once.
Each row is a math equation.
Each column is a math equation.
Remember that multiplication and division are performed before addition and subtraction.

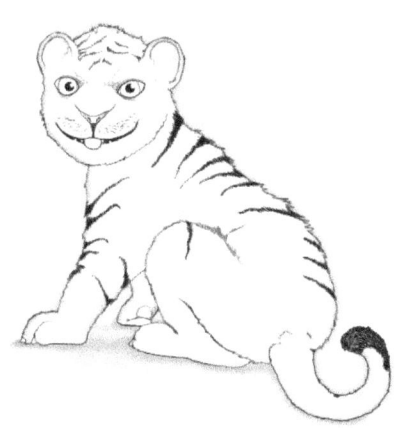

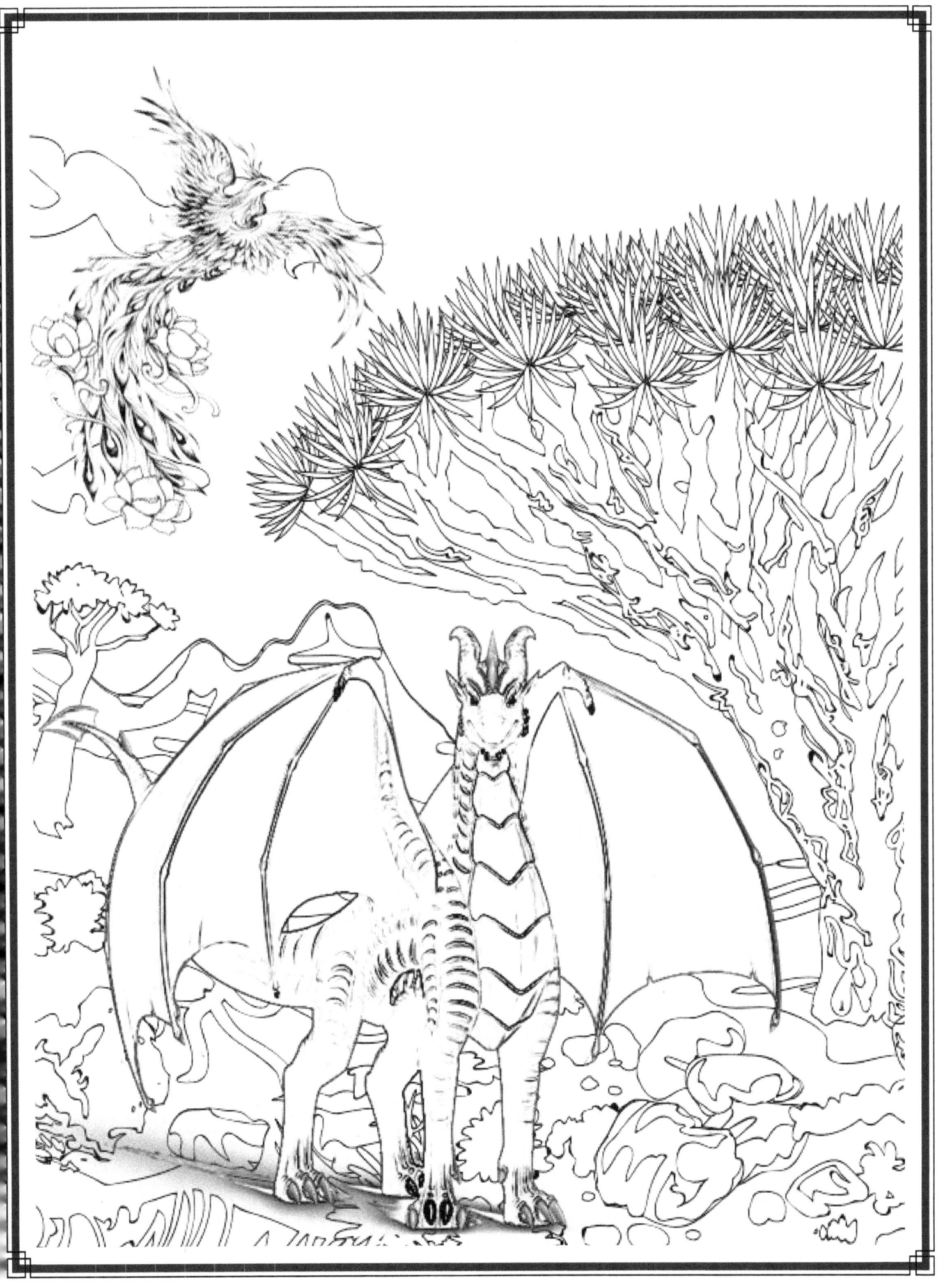

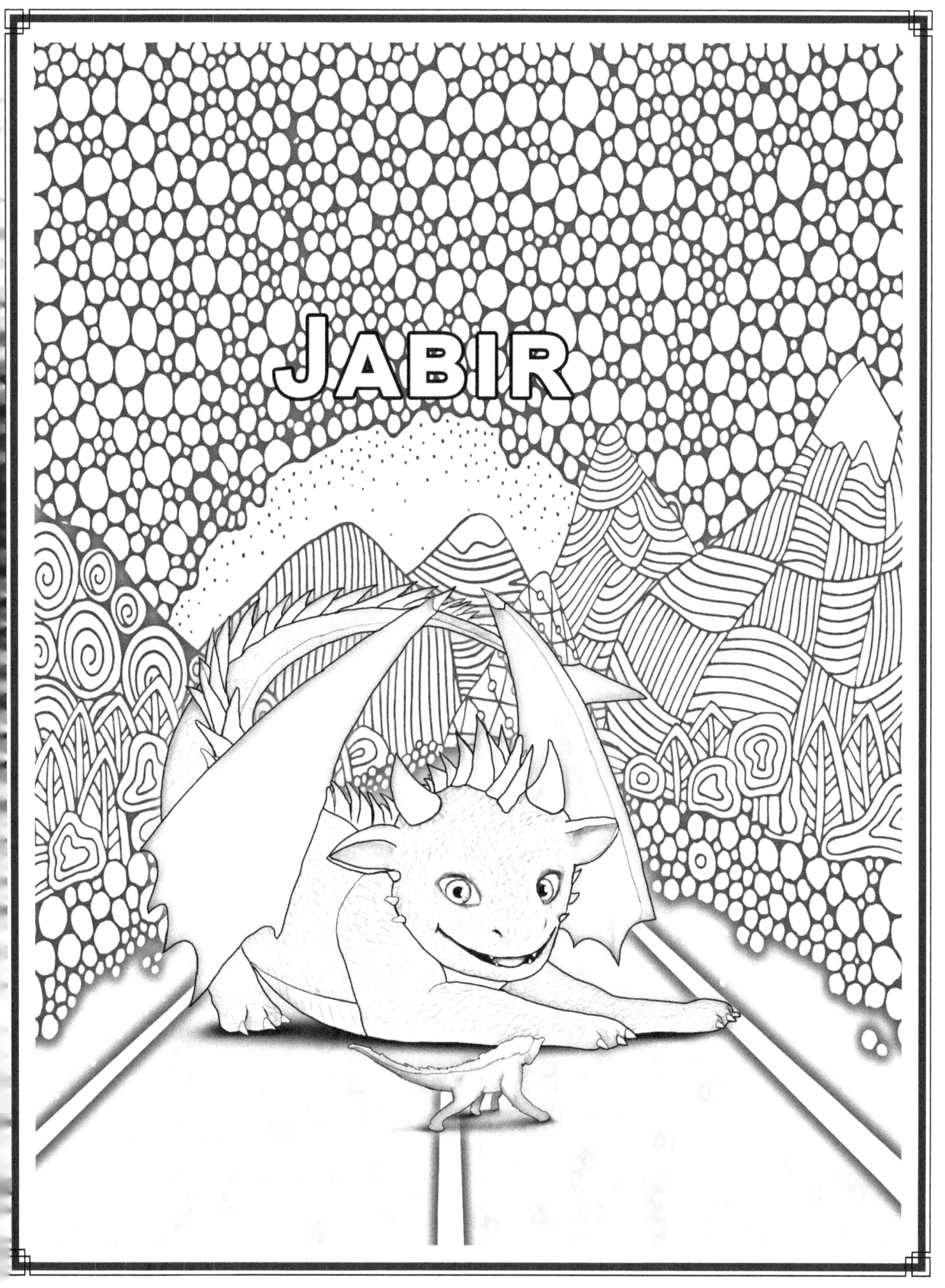

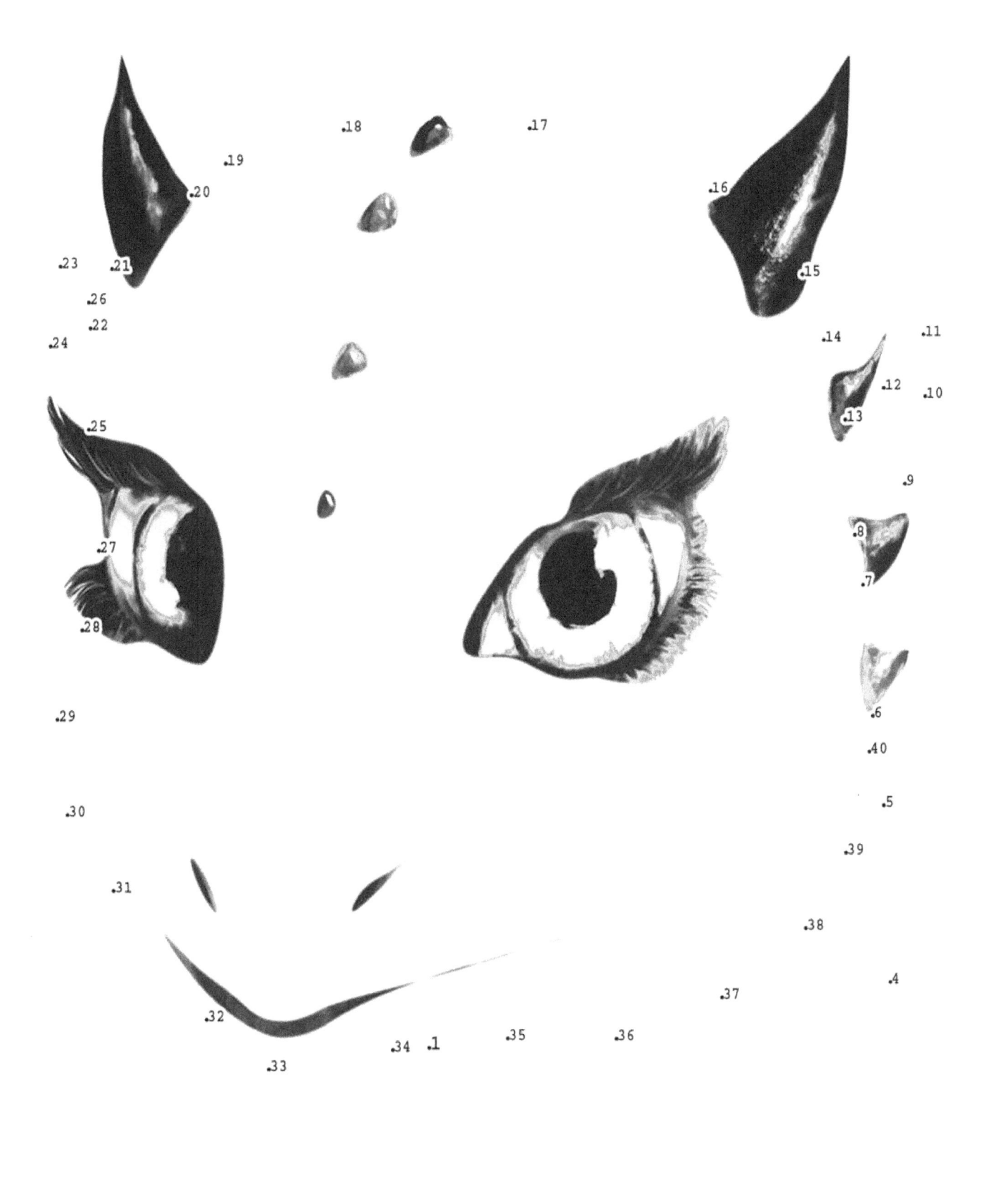

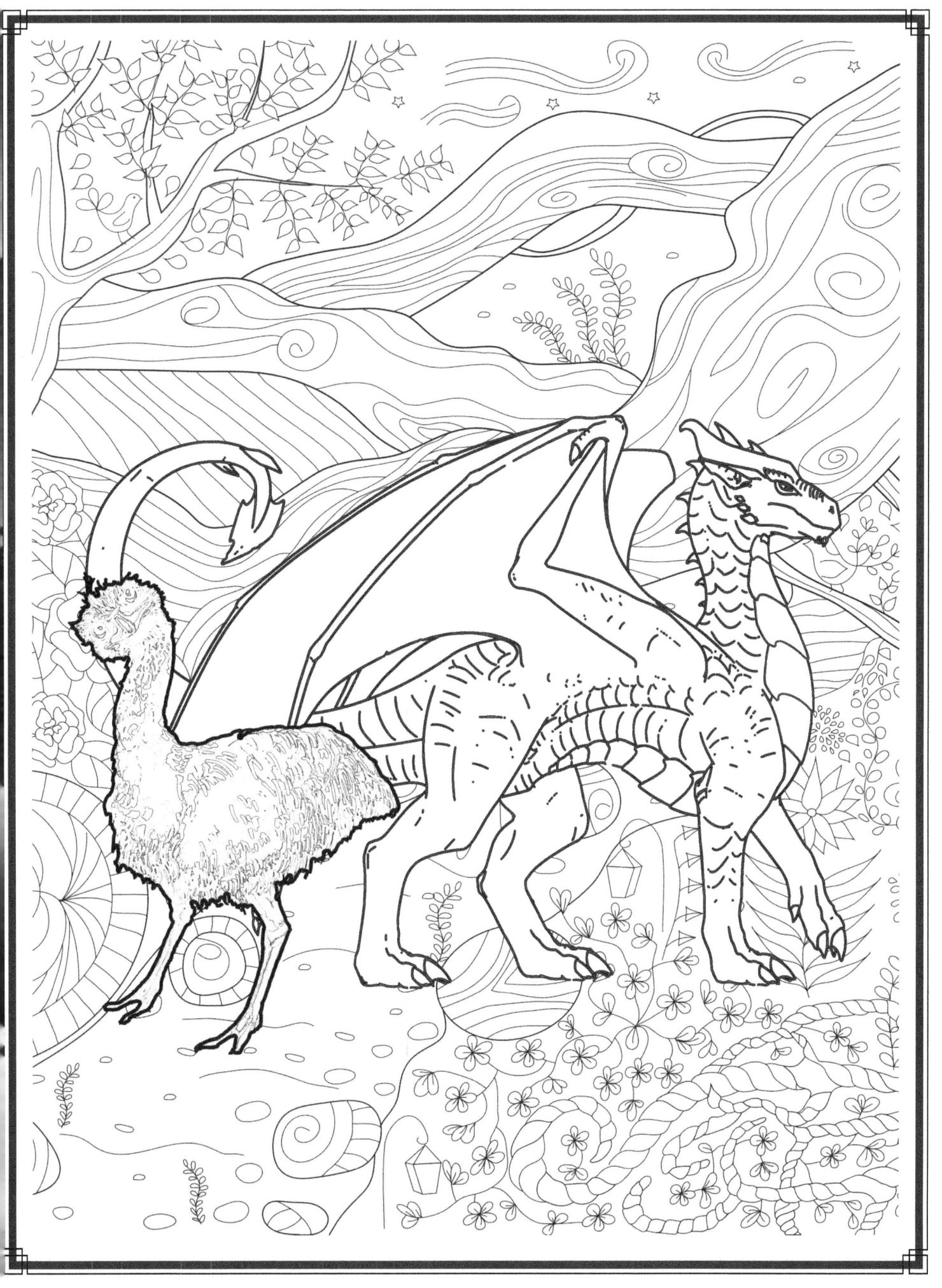

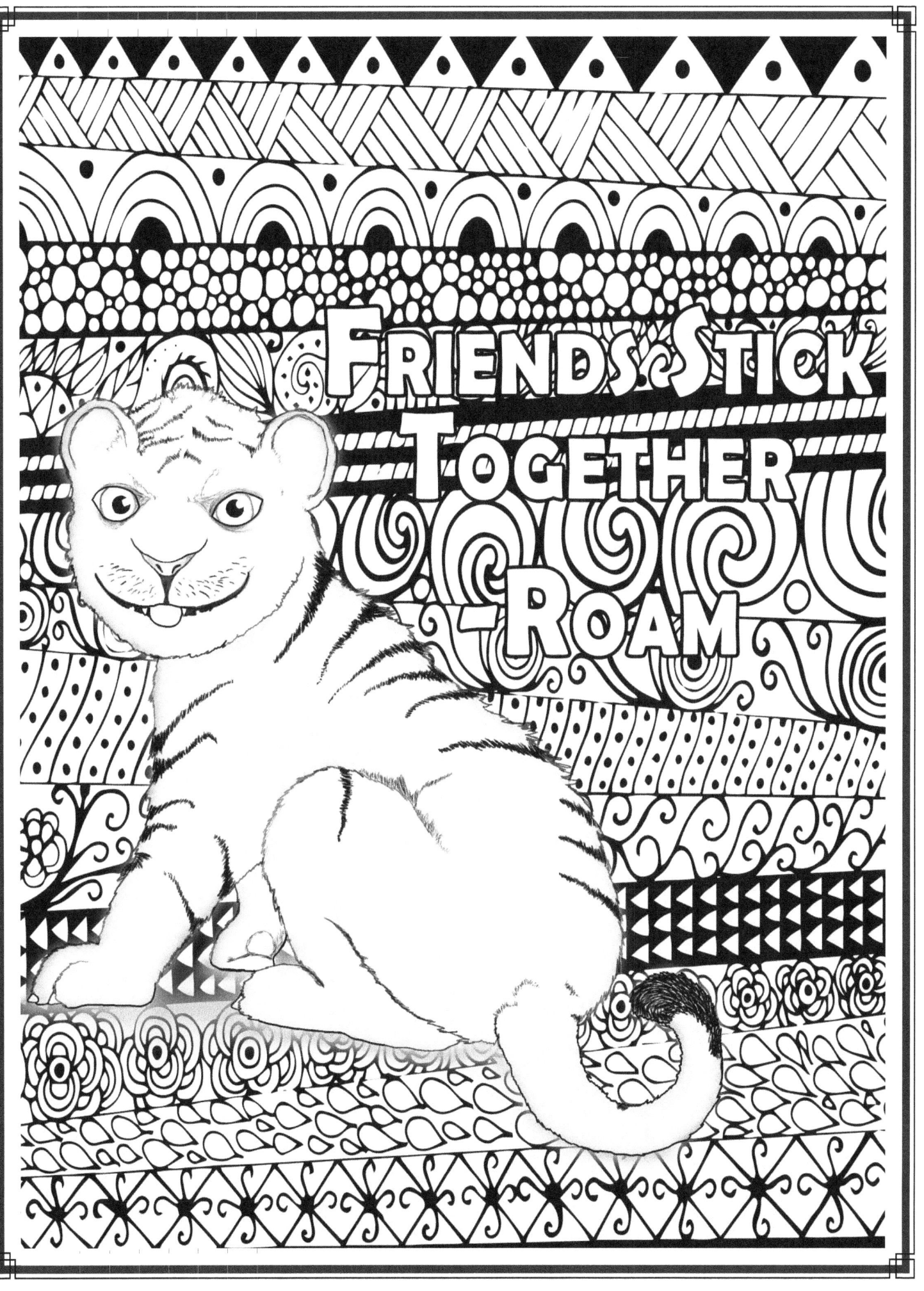

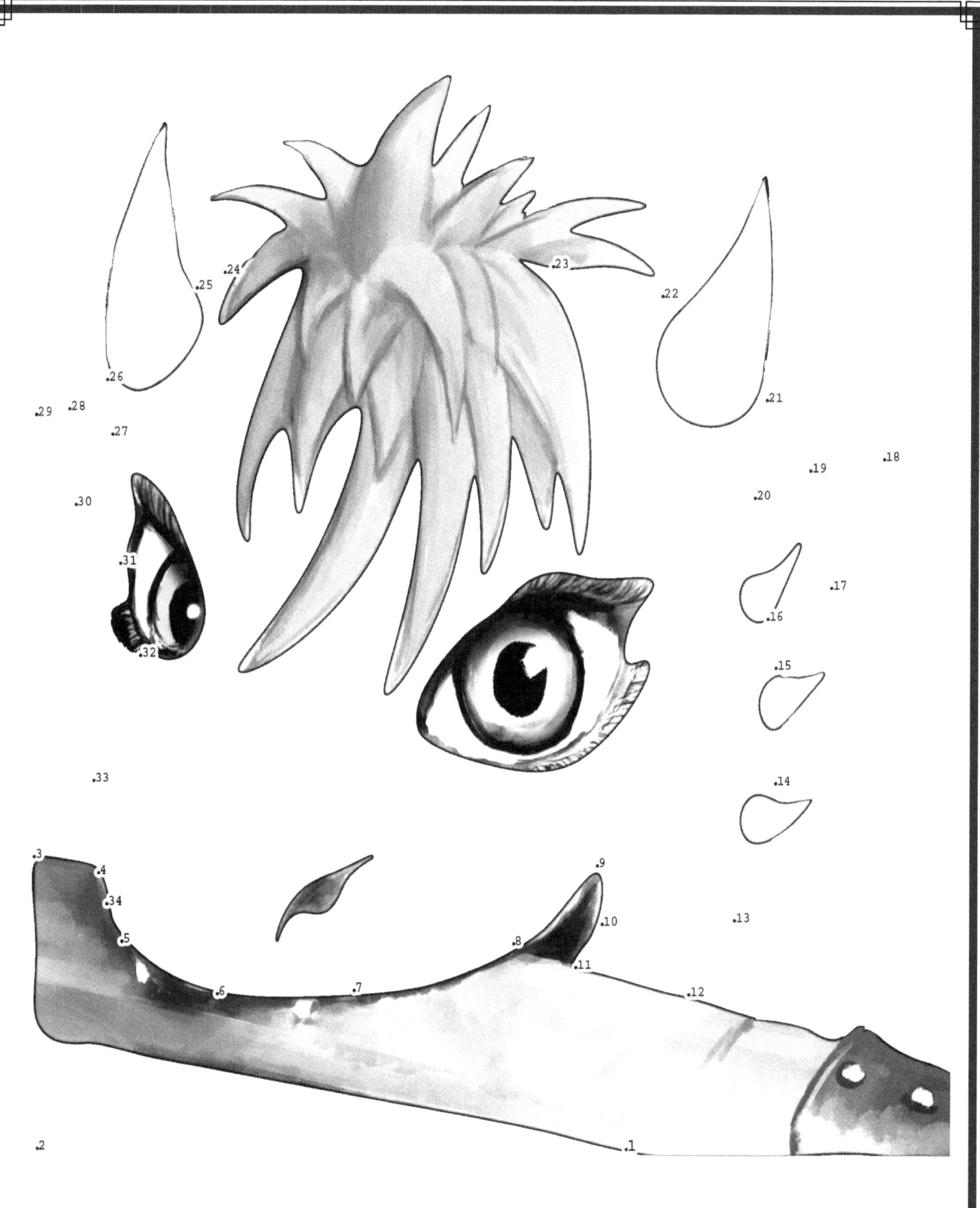

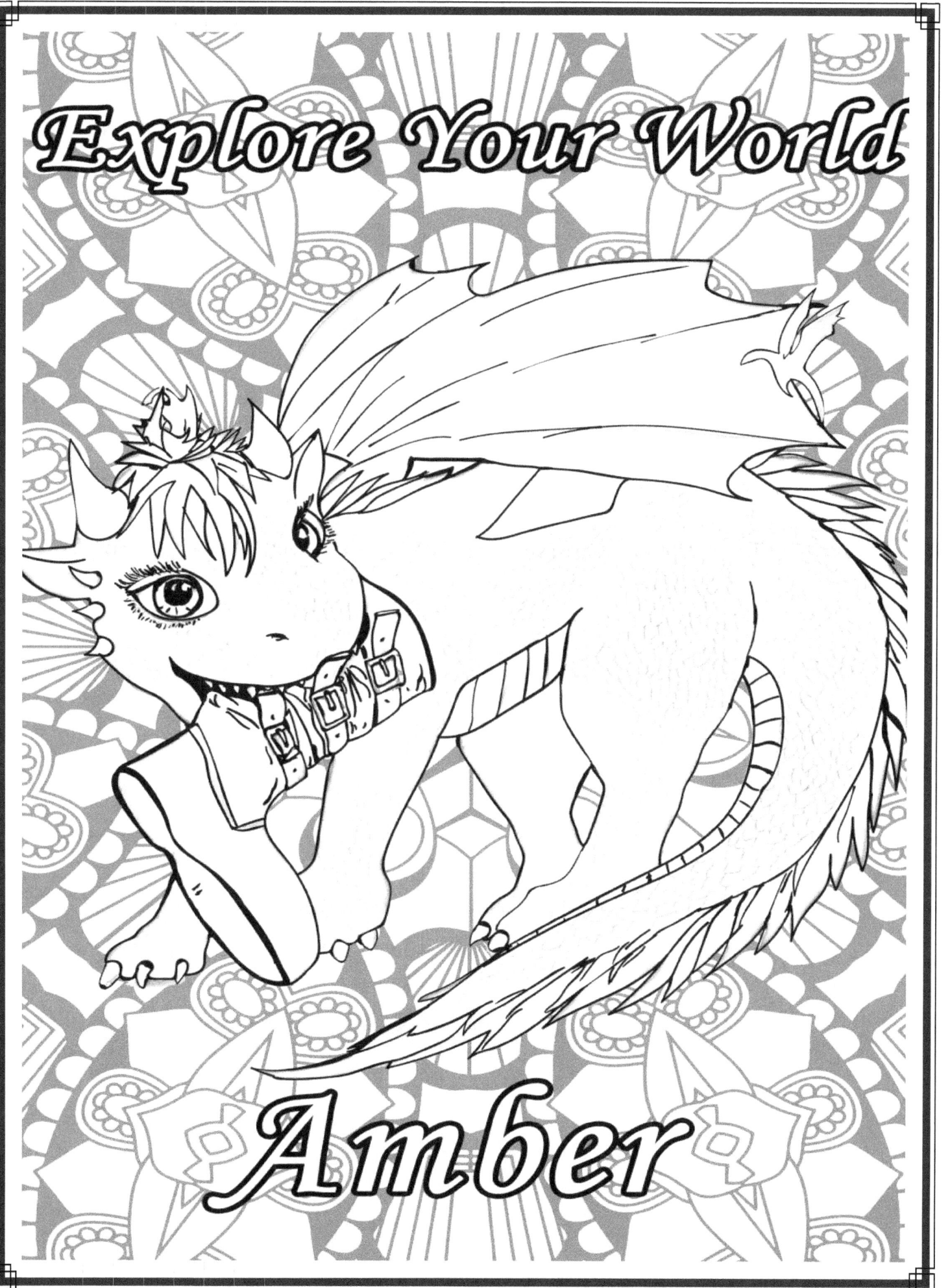

Roam

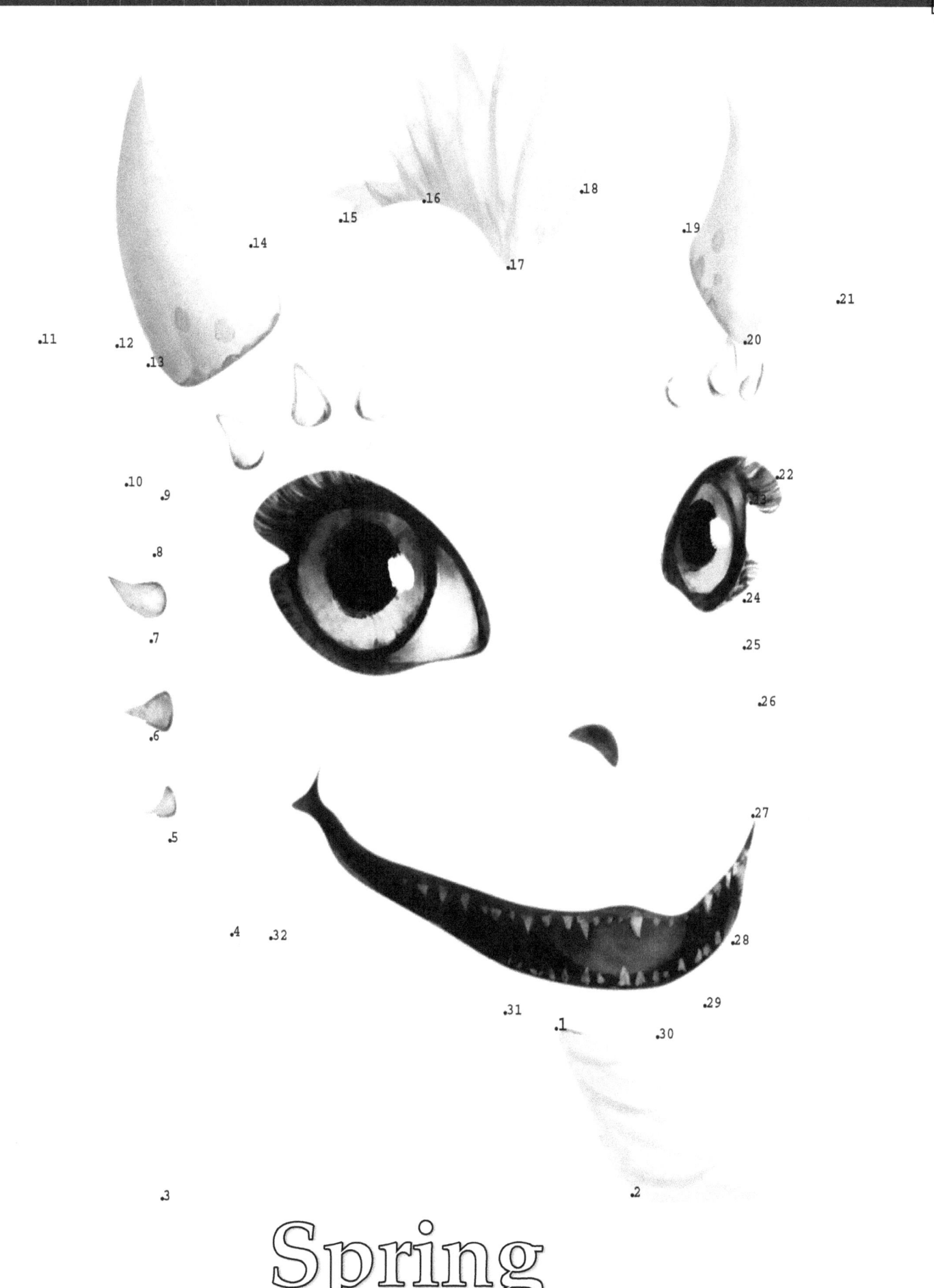
Spring

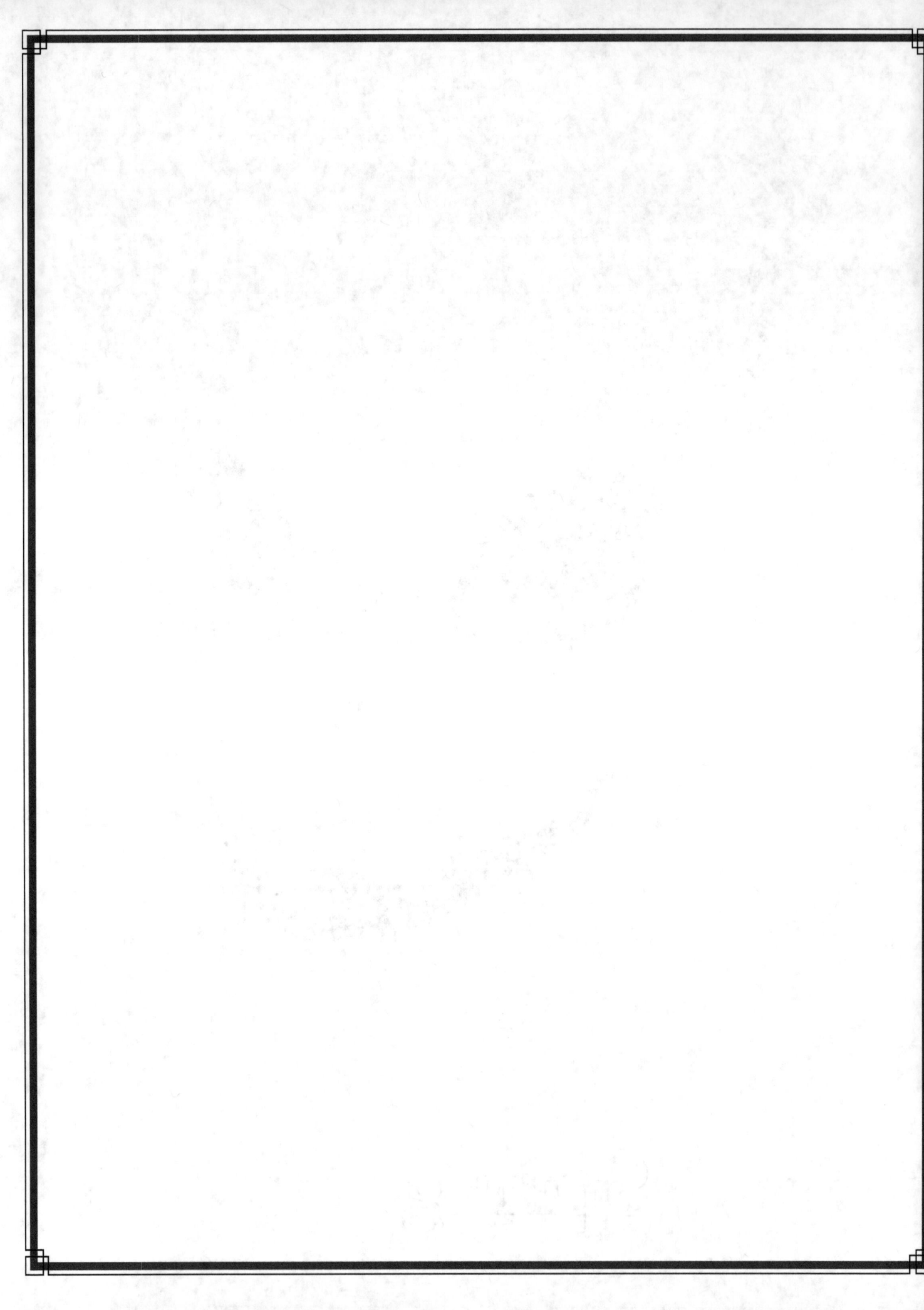

A Dragonling's Day at the Beach

A Dragonling's Day at the Beach

By S.E. Smith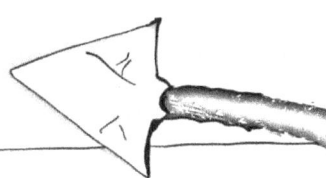

A Short Takes for Short Breaks Story

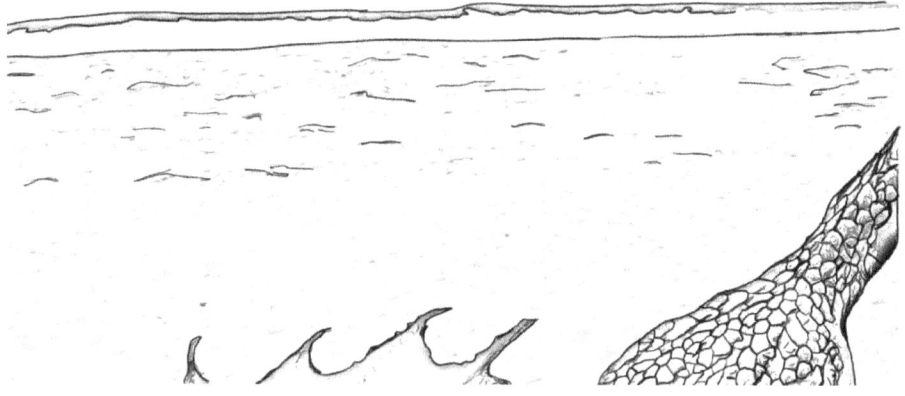

By S. E. Smith

Science Fiction Romance
A Dragonling's Day at the Beach
Dragonlings of Valdier Book
Copyright © 2015 by S. E. Smith
First E-Book Published July 2015
Cover Design by Laurelle Procter and Melody Simmons

ALL RIGHTS RESERVED: This literary work may not be reproduced or transmitted in any form or by any means, including electronic or photographic reproduction, in whole or in part, without express written permission from the author.

All characters, places, and events in this book are fictitious or have been used fictitiously, and are not to be construed as real. Any resemblance to actual persons living or dead, actual events, locales, or organizations are strictly coincidental.

Author's Note:

For those who have not read the Dragon Lords of Valdier, here is a little background.

The Valdier are dragon shifters. Only the Valdier and their mates can bond with the mysterious and powerful golden symbiots, who are, yes, symbiotic creatures, and they are stand-out characters all on their own! Each Valdier consists of three parts: the dragon, the man/woman, and their symbiot companion. They are friends with the Curizan (a species able to harness the energy around them) and the Sarafin (a cat shifting species). The following is a character guide for those new to the series:

Zoran Reykill,
Leader of the Valdier
true mate to Abby Tanner:
one son: Zohar
Zoran's symbiot: Goldie

Mandra Reykill
true mate to Ariel Hamm:
one son: Jabir
Mandra's symbiot: Precious

Kelan Reykill
true mate to Trisha Grove:
one son: Bálint
Kelan's symbiot: Bio

Trelon Reykill
true mate to Cara Truman:
twin daughters: Amber and Jade

Trelon's symbiot: Symba

Creon Reykill
true mate to Carmen Walker:
twin daughters: Spring and Phoenix
Creon's symbiot: Harvey
Phoenix's symbiot: Stardust
Spring's symbiot: Little Bit

Paul Grove
true mate to Morian Reykill:

Cree and Calo Aryeh
true mate to Melina Franklin:
one daughter: Hope

Vox d'Rojah,
King of the Sarafin
mated to Riley St. Claire:
one son: Roam

Viper d'Rojah
mated to Tina St. Claire:
one son, Leo

Asim true mate to Pearl St. Claire

Ha'ven Ha'darra,
Prince of the Curizan
mated to Emma Watson:
one daughter: Alice

Aikaterina: Unknown species; accepted as a Goddess to the Valdier, she is the oldest and most powerful of her kind.

Arilla and Arosa: Unknown species, still young for their kind, they are twins and thought to be Goddesses.

Trelon looked suspiciously at Amber and Jade. They had that look on their faces that said 'Perfect little angels', a term Cara had explained meant they were up to something. He raised an eyebrow when they both grinned at him.

A Dragonling's Day at the Beach

"Cara," Trelon called out in a slow, measured voice. "I think the girls are up to something again."

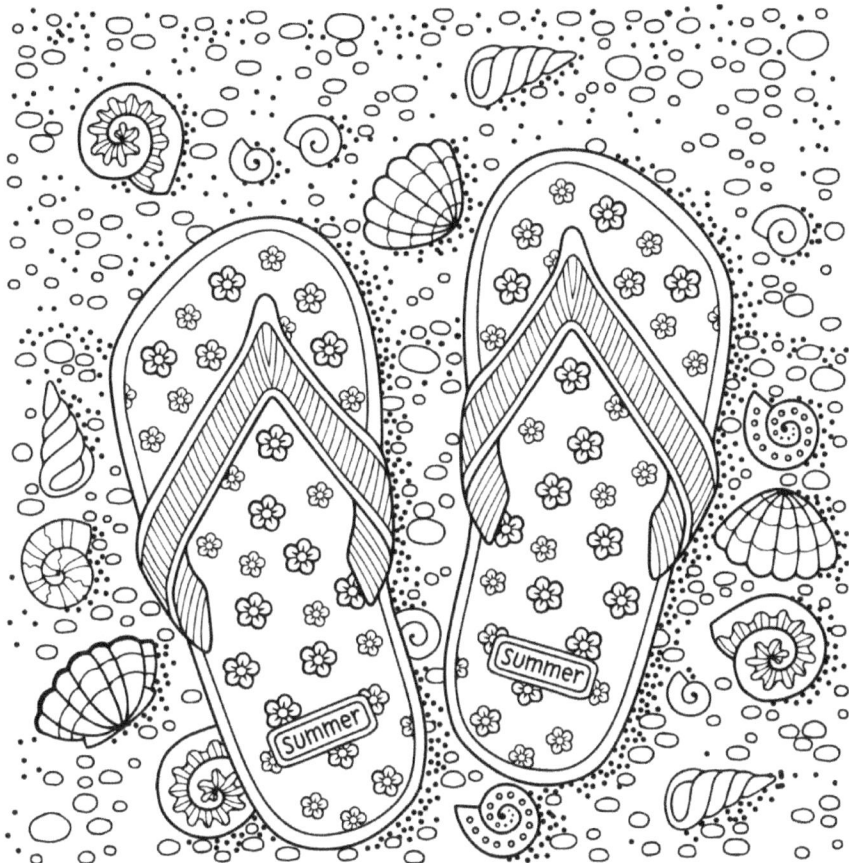

Cara's soft laughter echoed through their living quarters as she came out from the kitchen area. Trelon's suspicion grew when he saw both girls turn to each other and began talking in a frantic combination of hand gestures and garbled words that only they seemed to understand. He folded his arms across his chest and glared at Cara.

"What are they saying?" He demanded.

"They are saying you'd better get ready," Cara laughed. "Stop being so suspicious, they adore you, you know. I told them they had to be good if they wanted to go to the beach today."

Trelon ran his hand through his black hair. It was finally beginning to grow out. He knew they adored him. He was just suspicious because they were being extra well behaved this morning.

"Why are we doing this again?" Trelon asked, tilting his head at all the stuff by the door to their living quarters.

"We's goes swimming," Amber giggled.

"And's we's gets to plays in the sand," Jade added, grabbing her toes and wiggling them. "Momma's says we gets to bury you."

"But's we's not allow to eats the sands," Amber explained with a sigh. "Momma says its don't tastes goods."

"Bury…," Trelon turned to look at Cara again.

Trelon's heated glare melted when Cara walked over to him. He bent his head when she rose up on her toes to brush a kiss across his lips. A low purr escaped his dragon when she added a touch of her tongue to it.

"Not all the way," she whispered. "It will be fun."

Trelon released a sigh when Cara turned away and began picking up the items by the door. Both girls had shifted into their dragons and began bouncing up and down. Walking over, he gathered the chairs and a cooler. His eyes followed Cara and the girls as they headed down the corridor. Mandra, Ariel, and Jabir were at the other end. He glanced down at his symbiot which had shifted into a Werecat and picked up another bundle of items.

"I really need her to define 'fun'," he murmured to the golden creature looking up at him with an almost sympathetic smirk.

**

"Oh my," Carmen breathed, staring at Creon in the colorful shorts she had given him earlier.

Creon's eyes glittered with amusement and heat. He had been a little leery at first until he saw the two small strips of cloth that had been lying on the counter in the bathroom for Carmen. His eyes swept over the oversized cover she was wearing. He could see the straps of the material from earlier peeking out from the neckline. His body hardened at the thought of what was under it.

"Why's you's sticking outs?" Spring asked, breaking through his thoughts.

"What?" Creon asked in confusion, looking down to see his oldest daughter staring up at him, or rather at the front of his colorful shorts, with a puzzled expression on her face.

"You's undies moves," Spring said, gazing up at Creon. "My undies don'ts do that."

Creon flushed when he realized what Spring was talking about. He looked over to Carmen for help in explaining, but quickly realized he wasn't going to get any help from her when she covered her mouth with her hand to smother her laughter. He opened his mouth to try to explain, but snapped it shut when Phoenix spoke before he could.

"It's does that's in the mornings, too's," Phoenix commented. "Momma says we's don'ts have alls the sames parts as dada."

"But's I's wants to be's able to makes my undies sticks out, too's," Spring said, sitting down and pouting.

"I think I'll go see if Ha'ven needs any help," Creon muttered when Carmen burst out laughing.

"Chicken," Carmen giggled, walking over and scooping Spring up in her arms. "Let's get you two ready. Who likes purple?"

"I's do!" Phoenix said excitedly. "I's gets to wears purple today."

"I's wants yellow," Spring demanded. "I's loves yellow."

Carmen grinned at the relieved expression on Creon's face when the girls started to excitedly argue why their color was the best. She tilted her head when he came over to press a soft kiss to her upturned lips. He looked down when he felt a tug on the end of his shorts.

"You's growing agains," Phoenix informed him.

Creon bit back the burst of laughter and scooped Phoenix up into his arms. Turning, he glanced at Carmen again. There were some things about being a parent that he was totally clueless on how to handle. This was one of those times. When in doubt, hand it over to Carmen. That was the best way he knew when it came to dealing with things like this.

"I'll meet you down at the beach," he replied in a gruff voice as he handed Phoenix into her opened left arm.

"Chicken," she whispered again, watching as Creon hurried out of their living quarters. "Okay, time to pick out which swimsuit you want to wear," she said, turning her attention back to the two little girls in her arms.

"Can's we's uses Harvey to floats ons," Spring asked excitedly.

"Yes, I'm sure Harvey would love to be a float for you two," Carmen chuckled as she walked back to the girls' bedroom.

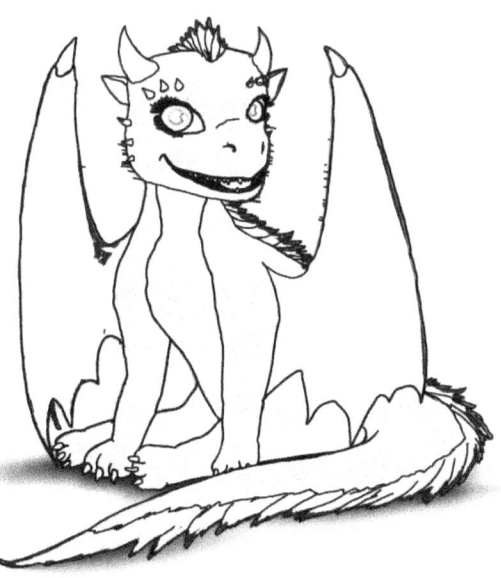
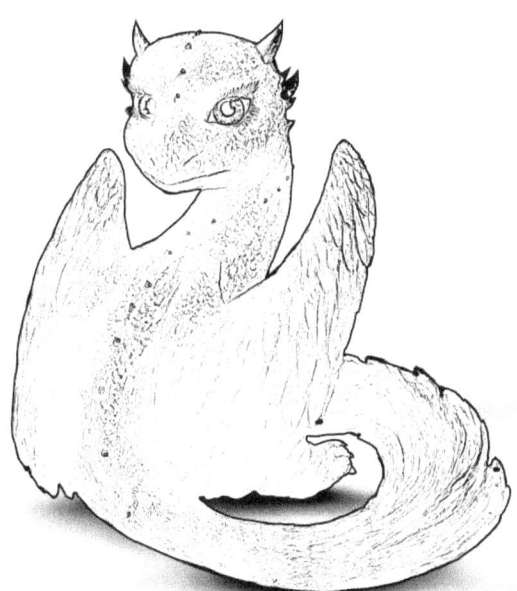

* * *

"I's needs this, and's this, and's this," Jabir said, pulling one toy after another out from under his bed. "And's I's really needs this."

"Jabir, I don't think you need all your toys for the beach," Mandra said in dismay, looking at the growing pile behind his son.

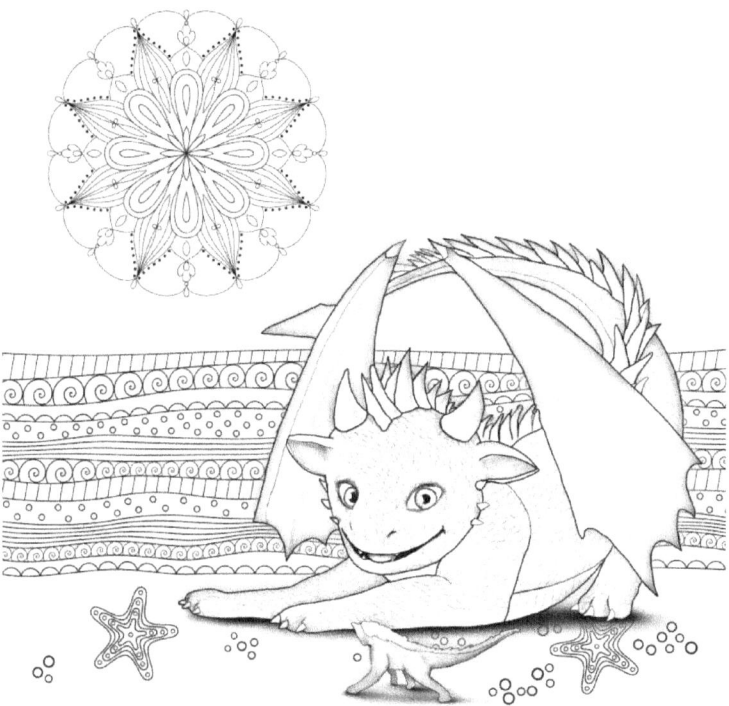

Jabir turned to look up at his dad with a frown before he nodded his head. "I's do's too," he said with a serious expression on his face.

"Ariel!" Mandra called, turning toward the door of Jabir's bedroom. "I's… I mean I need help!"

Ariel's husky laugh sent a shiver of need through Mandra. Shaking his head, Mandra groaned softly when his mind interpreted his body's reaction as 'I's needs this'. He ignored his dragon's soft chuckle as it stirred deep inside him.

Admit it, Mandra demanded. You were thinking the same exact thing.

Yes, I's needs her too's, his dragon admitted.

"What's the matter now?" Ariel asked patiently as she stepped into the room. "Oh!"

"Yes, oh's… I's… Dragon's balls," Mandra groaned, running his hands through his hair. "I'm talking like Jabir now."

"I's has some's dragon's balls," Jabir suddenly said, turning to gaze up at his dad. "See's!"

Ariel's uncontrollable laughter mixed with Mandra's sharp hiss when Jabir suddenly shifted into his dragon form. It wouldn't have been so bad except he had raised his little tail and showed them that he did, indeed have a set of dragon's balls. Jabir looked so proud, that Ariel had to turn her face into Mandra's chest as the laughter turned to uncontrollable mirth.

"I… Yes, you do's… do," Mandra muttered when Jabir shifted back again. "You's not helping the matter," he added under his breath to Ariel, even as his arms wrapped around her shaking body.

"I's knows," she teased, wiping the tears from her eyes. "It's just, if you could have seen your face… and Jabir… Oh, my."

Mandra's own chuckles mixed with Ariel's before they both drew in a deep breath. Turning to stare at the large pile of toys, Mandra rubbed his chin absently. He was always at a loss at how to deal with situations like this. He could tell a warrior 'no' in a heartbeat, but saying it to Jabir was almost as impossible as when he tried to say it to Ariel when she found a new 'pet'.

"Jabir, you can take two toys," Ariel said in a firm tone as she unwittingly came to his rescue again. "Remember, they are going to get sandy and wet, so you want to make sure they don't get ruined."

Jabir's eyes widened before he nodded. "I's takes my truck and boats."

"Perfect!" Ariel replied with a grin. "How about we get Precious to help you carry them down to the beach? Daddy can go help Ha'ven and Emma."

"And's Alice," Jabir said with a grin. "Bálint's likes Alice. I's do's too, but not's like Bálint. He's cans sees her colors."

"Yes, well," Ariel began, not sure how to address this new information. "I'm sure Alice likes you and Bálint, too."

"Uh-huh," Jabir said, pushing his truck with one hand and his boat with the other. "I's readys."

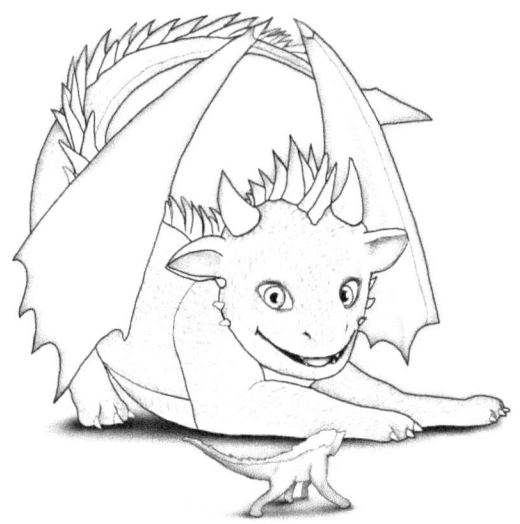

Ariel paused when Mandra's arms tightened around her for a moment. She looked up into his eyes and saw the glint of humor in them. Raising her eyebrow in inquiry, she tilted her head.

"Thank you for giving me a boy," Mandra whispered. "I'm not sure I could handle having a daughter just yet."

"Why not?" Ariel asked in surprise.

"Ask Trelon and Ha'ven," Mandra said with a grin.

Ariel's eyes widened when she remembered how Trelon swore he would never sleep again. He had been super protective of Amber and Jade when they were first born. It had only taken a few weeks before exhaustion, and Cara, had worn him out. It hadn't taken long for him to realize that he would never survive the girls, much less anything else, if he continued. Now, it was everyone else that he worried about. The girls were more than capable of taking care of themselves.

"You are terrible," Ariel whispered with a mischievous grin. "Well, there is no guarantee that we won't have a girl, so you'd better suck it up if we do."

Mandra paled and his eyes flew to hers. "You're not…?" He asked in a hoarse voice. "I would know…"

Ariel bent down and scooped Jabir up off the floor. Turning, she carefully placed him and his toys onto the golden saddle that formed on Precious' back. The symbiot turned its massive head to run a golden tongue up Jabir's cheek when he kicked his feet.

"Not yet, but I wouldn't be opposed to having another child," Ariel admitted with a tender smile as she ran her hand over Jabir's cheek.

Mandra's mouth dropped open as he watched Ariel, Precious, and Jabir walk out of the bedroom. His eyes lowered to the front of his colorful shorts. His body was saying a definite 'yes' to the idea.

Tonight I's going to have fun, his dragon crowed in delight.

A slow smile curved Mandra's lips as he glanced back at Ariel. The gentle sway of her hips started a fire inside him that was just as hot as the dragon fire. A low rumble of approval escaped him when she bent to pick up the beach bag she had packed.

I's is too, Mandra agreed with a happy grin. I's definitely is too.

..*

"Kelan, have you seen Bálint's…," Trisha's voice faded when Kelan stepped out of the bathroom with Bálint in his arms.

Her lips curved upward when she saw that Kelan had dressed Bálint in the swim shorts. They looked so much alike that it melted her heart. She walked over to where they were standing, grinning at her.

"I saw you had laid them out," Kelan said. "We couldn't wait, can we, Bálint? We got his toys all packed and sun protection on him. We're all ready to go, aren't we?"

"I's sees Alice today!" Bálint said with a grin. "I's goings to makes her sandy castles."

Kelan grimaced as he glanced at Trisha's amused face. "Yes, you'll get to make sand castles with Alice," he said with a wry grin. "And I'll get to watch Ha'ven glare at me all day."

Trisha chuckled and held her hands out for Bálint. "Is he still giving you the evil eye?" She asked with a grin.

Kelan nodded. "He was complaining that every time he, Emma, and Alice came to visit, something strange happens," he replied. "I told him there was nothing strange about going to the beach. There isn't, is there?"

Trisha turned and began walking toward their bedroom door. "No, there is nothing strange about going to the beach for the day," she laughed. "You guys act like this is the strangest thing in the world! Haven't you ever had a barbeque at the beach before?"

Kelan paused at the entrance to their living quarters and frowned. He thought back to his days as a dragonling. He didn't remember ever going to the beach to just hang out and play in the waves. He and his brothers and friends had sometimes played in the river and streams, but it was usually to cool off after they played their war games.

"No, not that I can think of," Kelan admitted. "So, why are we doing this again?"

Trisha rolled her eyes and opened the door. Kelan and Bio had already taken all of the beach stuff down to the cove where they were meeting the others. She was excited. There weren't any beaches in Wyoming and she had fallen in love with them when she was stationed in California. The water in the Pacific had been cold compared to the water here. The temperature here was more like that of the Atlantic side.

"It is a fun day to spend with family and friends," Trisha explained with an exasperated sigh. "You know, you can spend time with your friends without it involving war games and fighting."

Kelan frowned as he took the bag containing towels from Trisha's hand. "But, that is fun," he said in confusion. "It is also necessary to keep our skills developed."

Trisha looked at Kelan with an amused expression. "Yes, but now that you have a family, you can do other things as well. It will be fun. Besides, it gives me a chance to see you in those sexy shorts."

"I's sexy, too, mommy," Bálint suddenly said, pulling Trisha's face around to his. "I's wearing shorts."

"You are very handsome, just like your daddy," Trisha teased and dropped a kiss on the end of Bálint's nose.

"We's handy-some, daddy," Bálint said with a happy smile. "I's plays with my's friends. I's goes swimmy with you's, daddy. I's going to grows up strongs, justs likes you."

Kelan grinned and nodded. "Yes, you are," he said proudly.

Bálint gazed back at Kelan. "I's goings to's protects Alice," he added with a satisfied nod. "I's sees hers colors."

The smile on Kelan's lips faded and he turned his gaze to Trisha when she smothered a laugh. He scowled at her amused expression. He released an undignified snort.

"You laugh now," he muttered. "Just you wait. I've fought against Ha'ven in the wars. If you think he had something to fight for during it, you haven't seen anything yet. When it comes to Alice, he won't exactly be understanding that our son wants to mate with his daughter!"

Trisha glanced over her shoulder at Kelan's glum face. "They are kids," she reminded him. "I think we can hold off worrying about any wars or mating for a few more years."

Kelan nodded, but his expression didn't clear. "I'll warn the others just in case," he said with a frown. "I'll need to figure out a way to protect Bálint. Maybe I can take you both away somewhere…" His voice died when Trisha turned and stepped in front of him.

"We aren't going anywhere, there is not going to be a war, and will you please quit worrying about something that if it is going to happen, it will happen," Trisha said in a tender voice, laying her palm against her mate's cheek. "You know that if they are destined to be mates, there is nothing we can do about it. Besides," she added in a low voice. "I couldn't think of anyone else that would be perfect for our son."

Kelan's expression softened as he stared into Trisha's warm, brown eyes. "You're right," he admitted. "We have a few years before it becomes a problem."

Trisha chuckled and shook her head. Leaning forward, she brushed a kiss across Kelan's lips before stepping back. She rubbed her nose against Bálint's cheek, pulling a giggle from him.

"Sometimes your daddy drives me crazy," she whispered with a wink.

Bálint scowled at Kelan. "I's no shares my toys if you's drive mommy's crazys," he informed his dad. "I's the only ones that cans dos that."

Kelan's bark of laughter echoed in the corridor. He reached over and plucked Bálint out of Trisha's arms. Handing her the bag with the towels, he swung Bálint up onto his shoulders with a low growl.

"I guess we'll have to gang up on her," Kelan teased. "How about in the water? We can pretend we are ferocious dragons come to capture her all for ourselves."

"We's play tag?" Bálint asked in a hopeful voice. "I's gets to tag her firsts."

"Oh, we'll tag her, alright," Kelan said with a wink at Trisha as he started circling around her. "And when we capture her, we'll never let her go!"

"Yay! We's gonna captures mommy," Bálint chuckled, kicking his feet. "I's just likes my daddy."

Trisha shook her head as she watched Kelan and Bálint dance down the long corridor ahead of her. They were talking about how they were going to tag her and all the things they were going to do to her when they did.

Well, not all, she thought with amusement when Kelan pierced her with a heated look that woke her dragon up. We might have to be doing a little tag and capture ourselves, she added silently to her dragon.

I's likes that, her dragon purred.

Trisha couldn't keep the giggle from escaping as she hurried out of the palace after her two guys. Feeling younger and more carefree than she had in years, she raced down the path after Kelan and Bálint, uncaring of the low chuckles of the guards as she ran past them. Today, it was all about family and friends, but tonight… tonight it would be all about her and Kelan.

***

The sound of hushed whispers teased Abby, breaking through her concentration as she checked the bag full of towels, toys, and suntan lotion. She tilted her head and smiled. Zoran was trying to convince Zohar into his swimsuit. From the sound of the low growls, Zohar was having none of it.

Closing the top of the bag, Abby picked it up and carried it into the living room. She paused in the doorway, her eyes drawn to where Zoran was on the floor. His firm butt high in the air while the rest of his body was halfway under one of the end tables.

"Do you need some help?" She asked, leaning against the door frame and grinning when Zoran released a muttered curse after he hit his head on the table.

Zoran twisted until he was sitting on the floor next to the table. He absently rubbed his offended head while glaring up at Abby. His eyes flickered to the table before he returned his gaze to her and released a frustrated sigh.

"He is being stubborn," Zoran said with a slight pout. "It should not be this difficult to dress a youngling."

Abby chuckled. "He is going through a stage where he doesn't like to wear clothes," she explained. "All kids go through it. My grandfather used to tell me that when I was about Zohar's age every time he or grandma would dress me, I'd be stripping off the clothes the minute their backs were turned."

Zoran frowned and looked down at Zohar, who was peeking out from under the table at him. In a flash, the small dark brown and copper dragon raced toward Abby. Abby bent just as Zohar shifted and lifted him into her arms. She nibbled at Zohar's neck, pulling a giggle out of him.

"I's no wears clothes," Zohar stated, pulling back and looking at Abby with a fierce look.

"You will wear your swim outfit," Zoran said, rising up off the floor, the brightly colored piece of clothing in his left hand.

"No's. I's don'ts wants to," Zohar said, shaking his head.

Abby shot Zoran a sharp glance when he opened his mouth to argue with Zohar. "Why don't you want to wear your clothes, Zohar?" Abby asked in a calm voice as she walked over to sit on the couch.

"I's wants to be's likes dada," Zohar stated with a trembling lip.

Abby looked at Zoran in surprise when he knelt down in front of them. "But… Dada is wearing clothes?" Abby said in surprise. "See, he has colorful shorts and a shirt on just like what you have."

"Nots when's he's in the water," Zohar replied, his soft, golden eyes glittering with tears. "I's wants to goes in the waters and plays with the others."

"I'll be wearing my clothes in the water," Zoran said with a perplexed frown. "Why do you think I don't wear clothes in the water?"

"You's don'ts whens yous and momma's in the waters togethers," Zohar said with a hiccup. "I's wants to plays withs yous, too."

"When…," Abby bit her lip and gazed at Zoran when he looked at her with a puzzled frown.

"What is he talking about?" Zoran asked with an exasperated sigh. "When have we… Oh!"

"Yes, oh," Abby mumbled. "Momma and Dada will be wearing clothes down at the beach, Zohar, I promise. In fact, we might be wearing them in the shower for now on," she added under her breath.

Zohar looked back and forth between his mom and dad. A tiny frown darkened his eyes. He looked at the clothes his dad had on, before he turned in Abby's arms and wound his arms around her neck.

"I's wears clothes if yous do," he finally said.

"I think that is an excellent idea," Abby said, trying not to laugh at the look of resignation on her son's face. "The others will be wearing clothes, too."

Zohar turned back around in her lap and held his little legs out for his dad. Within minutes, he was dressed. Abby picked him up in her arms and hugged him close.

"Are you ready for the beach?" She asked. "I have some of your toys."

"I's ready," Zohar replied with a happy smile. "I's just like my dada."

Abby's eyes glittered for a moment when she thought of how hard-headed her son could be at times. She couldn't stop the curve of her lips when Zoran gave her a look that said he knew exactly what she was thinking. Shaking her head, she pressed a kiss to Zohar's cheek.

"Yes, you are," Abby chuckled. "You are just like your dada."

Zoran grinned at Abby and wrapped his arm around her waist, pressing a hot kiss to her neck. He nipped her skin just enough to let her know that he wouldn't be forgetting her little comment. He paused as he started to release her.

"We won't be wearing clothes in the shower," he whispered in a voice filled with promise.

··*

"Mama! I's can't finds my red swimmies," Alice hollered with a hint of despair in her voice. "I's needs help!"

"Alice, here is a blue swimsuit," Ha'ven said in exasperation, holding up the two tiny pieces of cloth. "Can't you wear blue today? It was your favorite color last week."

Alice sat down on the floor, crossed her arms, and pouted. "No's, I needs my reds one," she said stubbornly. "I wants my swimmies that's has ruffles."

"Here it is," Emma said with an amused grin at the blank look on Ha'ven's face. "It was still in the beach bag that Cara gave us."

Alice eagerly stood up and raised her arms up for Emma to pull off the red sundress she was wearing. "I's ready to goes," she said with a happy grin as Emma helped her into her swimsuit. "We's gonna have's fun."

Ha'ven watched as Emma turned Alice and efficiently tied on the bright red top. Shaking his head, he wondered what he had gotten himself into this time. When Emma said they were having a beach day, he had no idea that it was going to be the equivalent of moving their entire home. He glanced at the pile near the door to their living quarters at the Valdier palace; chairs, umbrellas, bags, a thing called an 'ice chest', toys, blankets, and other odds and ends sat next to it.

He started when he heard a knock on the door next to the pile. Striding over, he pulled it open. Creon and Mandra stood in the corridor with huge grins on their faces. Ha'ven's eyes widened when he saw what they were wearing. The feeling of dread and an uneasy sense of defeat ran through him at their expressions.

"What, may I ask, are you wearing?" Ha'ven asked in a slow measured voice.

"You can't go to the beach in leather, my friend," Creon said, pushing inside with a smirk. "These are called board shorts. They come in many different styles and colors. They are all the rage back on Earth with those that go to the beach."

"Emma," Ha'ven turned and started to protest in rebellion. His lips clamped shut when he saw her standing next to Alice holding up a pair of brightly colored shorts.

"You'd better hurry and change," she said with a slightly amused, but also pleading look. "Alice is so excited. This is her first trip to the beach."

Ha'ven ignored Creon and Mandra's sniggering as he slowly reached for the offending piece of cloth. Stepping close to his mate, he leaned down and brushed a kiss against her lips before whispering in her ear. This had to be up there with the most uncomfortable things he had ever done in his life.

"You are so going to owe me for this," Ha'ven growled softly before heading for their bedroom.

"We'll take your stuff down for you," Creon called out. "Everyone else is already there."

"Yeah," Mandra added, reaching for the chairs. "We're having a barbecue as well. This is going to be fun!"

"Why do I even bother to come here?" Ha'ven groaned as he disappeared into the other room. "Strange things happen whenever we do."

Creon and Mandra laughed as they gathered up everything but Emma and Alice. "We'll meet you down there. Don't be long. Cara is going to show us something called a boogie board."

* * *

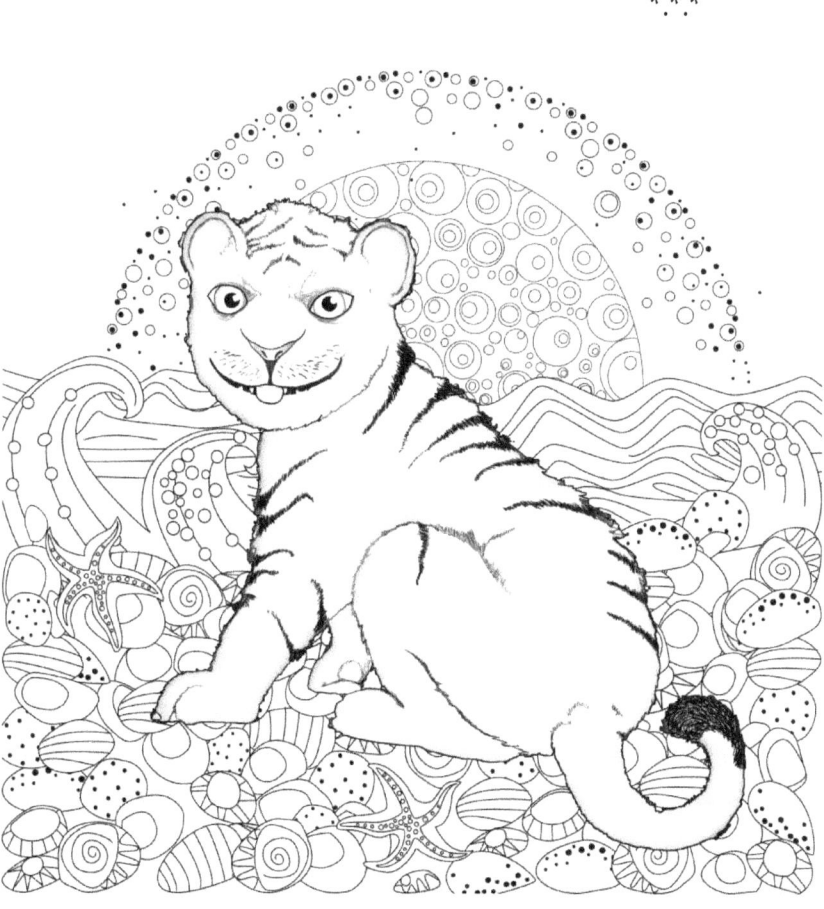

"Dam… Dang it, Roam, come back here!" Vox growled.

"Vox, are you ready yet?" Riley called out from the living room.

"Almost!" Vox snapped, dropping to his knees and staring under his and Riley's bed. A pair of bright blue eyes stared back at him. "Come on, Roam. I need those."

The little tiger cub growled and pulled further back under the bed, a pair of brightly colored board shorts hung from his mouth. His tiny paws were kneading the soft cloth even as he pulled on it. Vox's eyes glittered with determination. He should have known better than to tease his son with them.

"Vox, we're going to be late," Riley said, stepping into the room just as Vox was sliding under the bed. "You were teasing him again, weren't you?"

"He started it," Vox's muffled voice replied. "He said I couldn't catch him."

Riley raised an eyebrow and shook her head. How she won the lotto of having not one, but two kids – one big and one little – was beyond her. Folding her arms across her chest, she stared down at the long legs of her mate sticking out from under the bed.

With a soft whistle, she called to Roam. It was their signal for 'safe to come in' when they were playing games. Within seconds, the small white cub was trotting toward her with his dad's colorful shorts dragging behind him. Riley bent down and picked them both up just as a low curse escaped the man under the bed when he bumped his head.

"Daddy says damn," Roam laughed, dropping the shorts when he shifted in his mom's arms. "Damn, damn, dam…."

Riley quickly touched her fingers to Roam's lips and gave him a stern look. "Remember, we don't say that word anymore," she said with a small disapproving look. "Vox… "

"I know, Riley," Vox muttered as he scooted out from under the bed and sat up. "It slipped out. You've got my shorts," he added with a wry grin.

Riley used the tip of her foot to toss the board shorts she had ordered for Vox over to him. She had to tighten her hold on Roam when he tried to wiggle free to chase them. With a warning glance at Vox, she turned toward the door.

"I'll finish getting Roam ready while you change," she said, tossing a glance over her shoulder just in time to see Vox shrug out of the pair of leather pants he was wearing. "Oh lord," she breathed as a shiver of desire raced through her. Turning back around to the door, she slowly counted to ten as she walked out of the door and into Roam's room across the hallway. "Just… get ready."

"I saws daddy's…," Roam started to say before Riley interrupted him.

"What toys do you want to take down to the beach?" Riley asked in a slightly breathless voice as she sat him on the bed and reached for his swimming trunks. Sliding them on him, she tied the string in the front. "Do you want to take one of your trucks?"

Roam's eyes widened and he gave her a sharp-tooth grin. "I's wants my shovel and bucket," he demanded. "I's goings to burys Spring."

Riley rolled her eyes. Since Christmas, all Roam talked about was Spring. He was going to chase her and wrestle with her and eat bugs with her. Riley shuddered at the last one. Every time Roam mentioned eating bugs she wanted to go brush his teeth.

"Well, what do you think?" Vox's husky voice asked from behind her.

Riley glanced over her shoulder and almost fell over. Vox stood in the doorway wearing the board shorts and nothing else. A low hiss escaped her when he started flexing his muscles. Her eyes followed the movement.

"That ought to be against the law," she whispered, licking her lips.

Her eyes moved back to his and she was amazed that she didn't just self-combust as a wave of heat swept through her to pool low between her legs. From the look in Vox's eyes, she wasn't the only one affected by the heat in the room.

"Mommy, Mommy," Roam said, patting Riley on the cheek.

"Wha… What, honey?" Riley asked, turning back to where Roam was sitting on the bed.

"I's says I's ready," Roam said again. "I's wants to goes bury Spring and plays with Jabir and Bálint."

Riley cleared her throat and nodded. "Yes, I think that is a marvelous idea, the playing with Jabir and Bálint, not the burying Spring," she replied, pushing up off the floor.

"You need to take it easy," Vox muttered, wrapping his arm around her when Roam jumped into her arms.

Riley shook her head in exasperation and leaned back against Vox's broad chest. Another shiver ran through her as the heat from his skin pressed against her back. She barely held back the curse that almost escaped her when she felt him do the man-boob thing again. He was feeling frisky today! That invariably meant trouble, usually for her.

"Are you going to be doing the boob-bounce all day?" She asked in a husky voice, turning in his arms.

"I's does the booby-bounces," Roam announced before he looked at his dad with a frown. "What's booby-bounces mean?"

"They are not boobies," Vox scowled.

Riley choked back a laugh when Vox flushed. "And that, my dear mate, is why we need to watch our language around Roam."

"I think it is time to go," Vox muttered, plucking Roam out of Riley's arms and tossing him over his shoulder. "I've got me a cub to dunk in the ocean."

"I's don'ts likes water!" Roam hissed. "I's gots to burys Spring."

Riley rolled her eyes as the two kids – one big and one little – argued over whether or not cubs liked water. Her hand moved instinctively to her stomach when she felt the slight flutter in it. At least she had some re-enforcement on the way.

Just wait, she thought with a mischievous grin. Before long, the girls were going to outnumber the guys. When that happened, Vox would really be wondering what hit him.

* * *

Tina looked down at the group spread out on the beach. She turned when she felt an arm wrap around her waist. Viper stood staring down at the group with a wary look on his face.

"You're the one that told your brother you would go," Tina reminded him. "I suggested that we make a graceful retreat in the middle of the night."

Viper grimaced at the reminder. He should have taken Tina up on her offer. He would have if he hadn't been curious about what a 'Beach Day' was all about. If it was half as fun as the Christmas one turned out to be, he hadn't wanted to miss it. It wasn't every day that he had the chance to see the King of Valdier hanging upside down from a tree like a drunken bird.

"I've never been to a beach day," Viper muttered. "Vox said there would be plenty of food."

Tina shook her head. "You wanted to try out the boogie board and build sand castles," she retorted with a raised eyebrow. "You talked in your sleep last night."

Viper gave her a sheepish grin. "It sounds like fun," he admitted.

"It is," Tina reluctantly agreed.

Viper started, turning her so he could stare down at her with a look of suspicion. "You know how to do these things?" He demanded.

"Duh," she replied, looking up at him as if he was dense. "I'm human and lived on the coast of California. Of course, I know how to do it!"

Viper's jaw tightened into a determined line. "You will show me," he insisted. "I want to learn to build this castle out of sand. Do you use a machine? How big is the castle? How do you make the walls secure so they do not collapse? I saw the boogie board that Cara made. How can it carry a body on it? Why do humans like to ride on them? Is there any…"

Tina pressed her lips against Viper's. It was the only way she could think of to shut him up. A low groan escaped her when his arms slid around her and pulled her closer to his body. It took the sound of a throat clearing to finally bring them back to the fact that they were standing in the middle of the path leading down to the beach.

"Hi, sis," Riley said in a cheerful voice. "I never figured you as a beach bunny."

"Shut up, Riley," Tina groaned, glaring at her older sister.

Riley's husky laugh echoed in the wind. "Never," she retorted. "So, are you coming or going?"

"Tina is going to show me how to make castles out of sand before demonstrating how to boogie on a board," Viper explained with a wry grin.

"My's daddy has booby-bounces," Roam informed Viper and Tina with a grin. "I's saws him."

"O…kay," Riley said with a huge, fake grin. "Who wants to be buried in the sand?"

Tina watched as Riley, Vox, and a grinning Roam hurried down the path to the beach. She shook her head. She wasn't sure she wanted to know just what the hell 'booby-bounces' was. Glancing at Viper, she had a feeling that was going to be another question he would want answers to before the day was over.

"I'm so glad that we don't have any kids," she muttered.

"At the moment," he replied with a mischievous grin before he headed down the path after his brother, Riley, and Roam.

Tina stood staring blankly at Viper. What did he mean 'at the moment'? Did he think that they were going to have a…

It take you long enough, her cat muttered, stretching inside her. Why you think we so tired lately?

"Oh, shit," Tina whispered, staring at Viper's knowing grin. "You… Viper!"

∴

Jabir raced over to where Roam's dad was setting him down on the ground. With a low growl, the two friends tumbled in the soft sand. They played for several minutes before Jabir looked down the beach.

"Looks!" Jabir exclaimed, pointing at the moving mound of sand coming at them. "What's that's?"

"I's don't knows, but's I's going to gets it," Roam growled, shifting into his tiger.

Jabir watched as Roam bent down, his tail flickering back and forth as they watched the moving pile of sand approach them. Jabir watched with wide-eyes as the moving pile grew closer and closer. He opened his mouth to call out a warning when Roam pounced.

A loud, startled hiss escaped Roam when Spring suddenly appeared in front of him. He fell to the side and rolled across the sand before crawling back to his feet. Shaking, he flung sand all over Jabir before he snorted when Spring grinned at him.

"I's scared you," she crowed.

"You's did not," Roam said, shifting and wiping his hand across his face. "I's knew it was you all the time."

"No's you didn't," Spring said with a grin before she turned and looked up at where Phoenix, in the shape of her dragon, was landing at the edge of the water where it rolled to shore. "Last's ones ins has to eat bugs."

Roam growled and took off after Spring, forgetting that cubs were not supposed to like going in the water. Jabir laughed and followed them. Amber and Jade were already splashing in a tidal pool. The moment the boys got there, the three girls shifted and tackled them. Loud screams of delight resonated throughout the cove as the kids splashed and played.

∴

"Oh, my," Abby whispered, her eyes locked on Zoran.

"What?" Cara asked, turning to look at where the men were standing around the portable grill she had built. "Oh, yeah!" She breathed out, her eyes glued on Trelon.

Ariel stepped closer to Abby and Cara and fanned herself. "I swear the temperature has just risen a hundred degrees. Have you ever seen so much muscle on any beach before? It would cause a riot back home. Damn, but that man makes me hot," she muttered as her eyes swept over Mandra's huge form.

"There should be a law that states men like that are only allowed to wear board shorts," Carmen chuckled.

"Or Speedos," Riley added with a raised eyebrow. "Can you imagine them in those tight little pieces of spandex?"

"Oh yes," Emma said, blushing when the other women turned around and looked at her in surprise. "I'm artistic. I have a very good imagination."

Abby laughed and nodded. "You and me both, Emma."

Trisha turned mischievous eyes to the women. "How about we see if they are as impressed. I swear Kelan is flexing his muscles on purpose."

"Oh, Vox has been doing that pectoral bounce with his man-boobs ever since he came out of the bedroom. I swear if I could get my boobs to do that, they'd knock me out," Riley replied with a sigh. "The man knows he is too sexy for himself."

"Viper's the same way," Tina replied, grinning at her older sister. "He thought I was nuts when I asked him to wear the shorts until he saw what I was going to wear."

"Well, I think we should show them just how sexy we are," Carmen replied with a smug grin. "I've got boobs now I didn't have before the girls and I'm not afraid to flaunt them."

In a matter of minutes, the colorful swimsuit covers were lying on the backs of the chairs the women had arranged in a straight line facing the kids. While the women chatted and kept an eye on the kids, the men were supposed to be figuring out how the grill Cara built worked so they could 'grill' the meat and vegetables for lunch.

"I never…" Carmen's voice faded on a gasp when a pair of arms swept around her. "Creon!"

"You didn't show me this… clothing before we left!" He growled, sliding his mouth along her neck.

Carmen giggled and rolled her eyes. "That's because I had a feeling we'd never make it to the beach if I had," she responded in a husky voice. "I thought you were supposed to be helping the guys cook lunch."

"Ah, Carmen, I don't think any of them are thinking about cooking," Trisha said in a breathless voice.

Carmen glanced over and shook her head. Sure enough, each of the women had their hands full, and it wasn't with the kids. Turning in Creon's arms, she wound her arms around his neck and released a sigh.

"If it helps," she whispered with a slow sexy smile. "You are just as distracting to me."

"Yews…," a chorus of young voices groaned. "They's kissing agains."

Laughter echoed through the air. After several fruitless attempts to redirect the men back to the grill, Cara finally suggested boogie boarding lessons for the men. Fascinated by the idea, it wasn't long before the men were competing to see who could stay on the longest. The kids, not wanting to be left out, insisted they needed to ride, too.

Abby looked up when a shadow covered her. Zoran, dripping wet and grinning ear to ear. He sank down beside her and Zohar. He stared at the intricate castle she was building for several long seconds before he smoothed a section on the outer wall.

"What are you doing?" He asked, watching as Zohar began digging in the sand.

"Making sand castles," Abby replied with a grin. "I loved it when I was a child. Now, I get to do it with our son."

Zoran glanced over at where Trelon was being buried alive by Amber and Jade. Cara just grinned and told the girls they had missed a spot. Cara, Ariel, and Trisha had finally taken over the grill.

"Just make sure he can breathe," Cara added when Amber climbed up on Trelon's sand covered chest to pat it down.

Once again, he was thankful he had Zohar and not the twins. Turning, he watched as Mandra and Jabir chased tiny 'crabs' as Ariel called them. They weren't very tiny and from Mandra's smothered curses, neither were their claws. Yet, Mandra was determined to catch one for Jabir.

Creon and Carmen were still in the water with Phoenix and Spring, while Riley, Vox, and Roam, along with Viper and Tina, were exploring a rock cave at the end of the beach. Emma, Alice, and Bálint played in the small tidal pool.

"It's a shame Melina, Cree, and Calo couldn't come," Abby said, pouring water into the moat that she and Zohar had dug. "It is Cree and Calo's parents anniversary and they were having a party for them."

Zoran turned back to stare at Abby's glowing face. "Then we will have to plan another 'beach day'," he said with a smile. "I never realized how much fun they could be."

"Hel… Help…," Trelon's muffled voice called out. "I think one of Jabir's damn crabs has gone down my shorts!"

"Ohhh!" Amber and Jade laughed. "It bites daddy on the…"

"Girls!" Cara yelped, handing the spatula to Trisha.

Trisha and Ariel grinned as they watched Cara frantically try to unbury her mate.

"Damn, but I love the beach," Ha'ven said with a grin as he and Kelan watched Trelon jump up and down from where they were sitting under one of the umbrellas.

"The scenery isn't bad either," Kelan said, watching as Trisha bent over to get something out of one of the ice chests.

"No, it isn't," Ha'ven agreed with a contented sigh as he watched Emma throw her head back and laugh. He smiled when she suddenly turned her head and looked at him, as if she knew he had eyes only for her and Alice.

I love you, she whispered silently to him. *Thank you for doing this.*

I love you, too, he replied with twinkling eyes, running his eyes over her exposed skin. *Beach days are not as bad as I thought, but you are still going to owe me.*

Anytime, Emma said with a hot look of her own. *Anytime.*

* * *

No one saw the three golden figures floating high above the group. Two of the figures giggled and pointed at the men, women, and children that played far below them. The other figure watched with a sense of curiosity and amusement.

"Aikaterina, do you think we might try to do that?" Arosa asked in a voice laced with excitement.

"Oh, yes," Arilla said. "It does look like fun."

Aikaterina's lips curved upward as one of the men took a tumble off the narrow board he was riding. She had to admit, it did look like… fun. The strange sensations she had been experiencing lately shifted inside her again. It had been occurring more frequently since she had first made contact with the humans. Both the male and the females of the species were unusual. They made her… curious.

"Yes," she replied with a wave of her hand. "But remember not to lose track of time."

"We won't," Arosa promised. "Come, sister, I know a cove where we can try this."

Aikaterina didn't bother to turn as the two sisters next to her floated away. She was too fascinated by the interactions below her. Her eyes followed one couple as they walked down the beach. Their hands were entwined and they appeared to be talking. The male was talking quietly to the female. When they reached the end near the cave at the end of the cove, the female turned and nodded.

"I wonder," she whispered, watching as the man drew the woman into his arms and pressed his lips to hers. Aikaterina's hand rose to touch her lips. "I wonder what it would be like to be held like that."

With a shake of her head, she let her body dissolve so that it was no more than a mist. Focusing, she created a small breeze that would carry her back to the Hive. She could have journeyed there with just a thought, but for some reason, she wanted to remain out among this world just for a moment longer. Closing her eyes, she imagined what it would be like to be held… to be… loved.

For more stories, check out the **Additional Books and Information** at the end of this book!

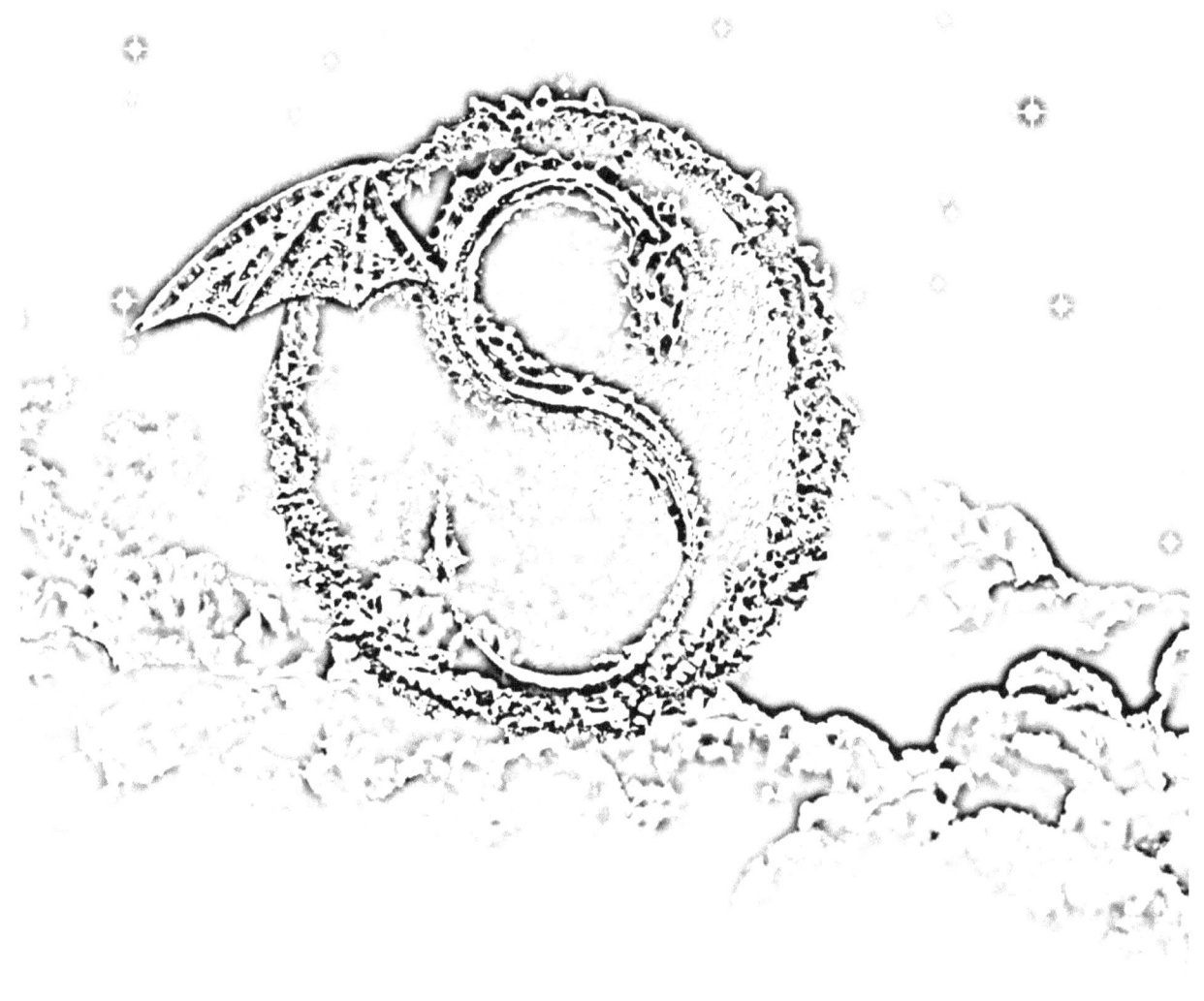

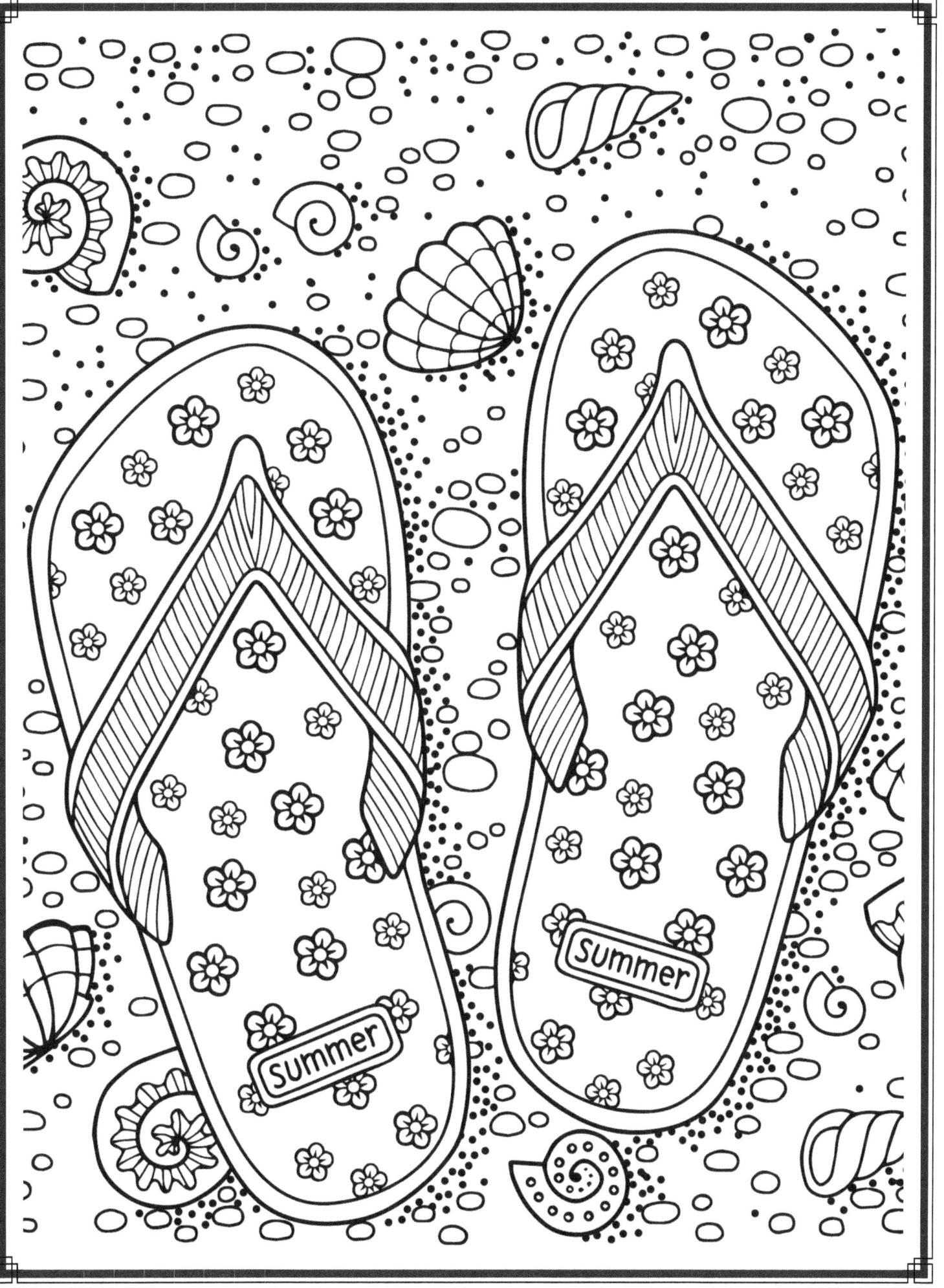

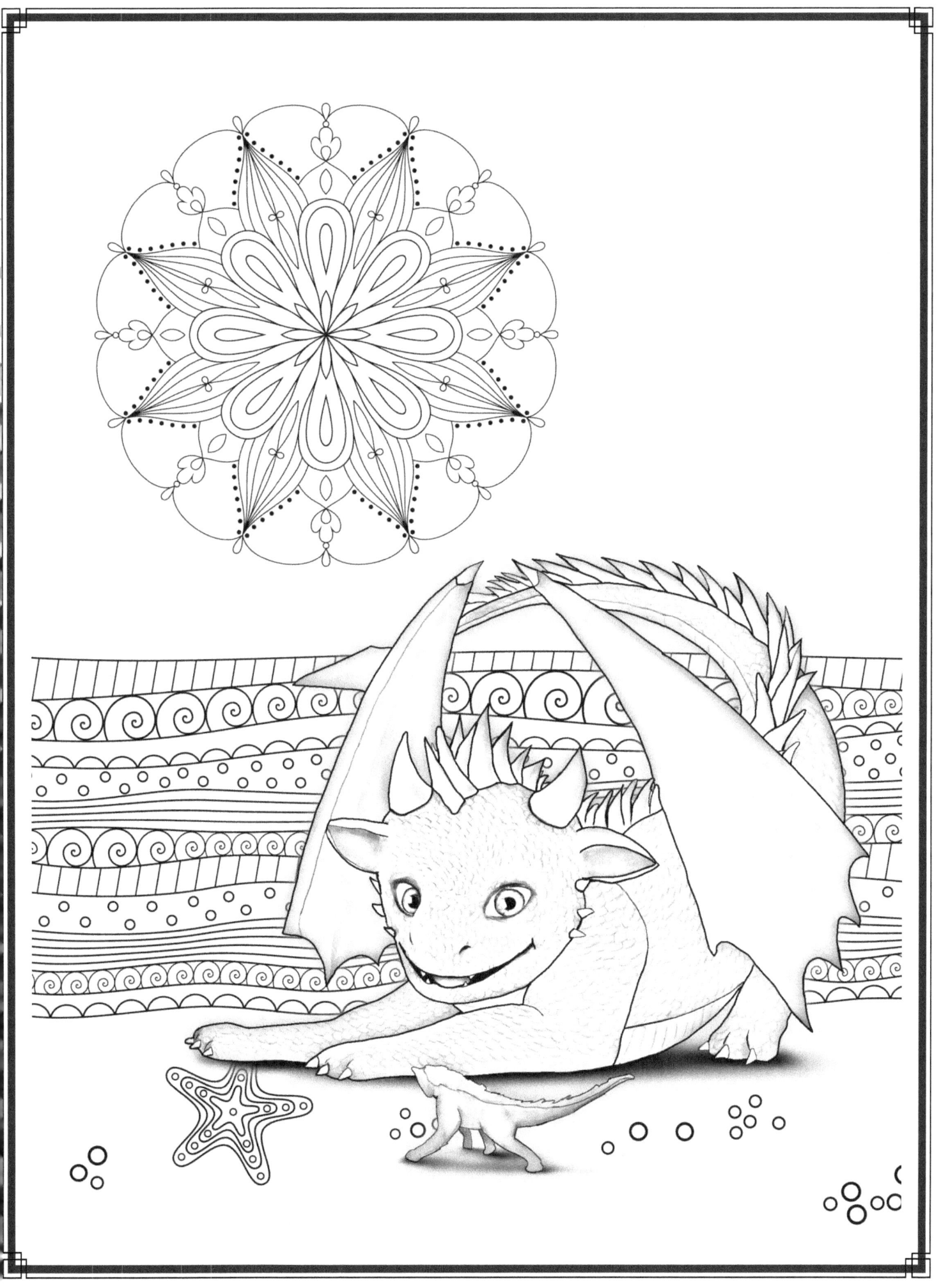

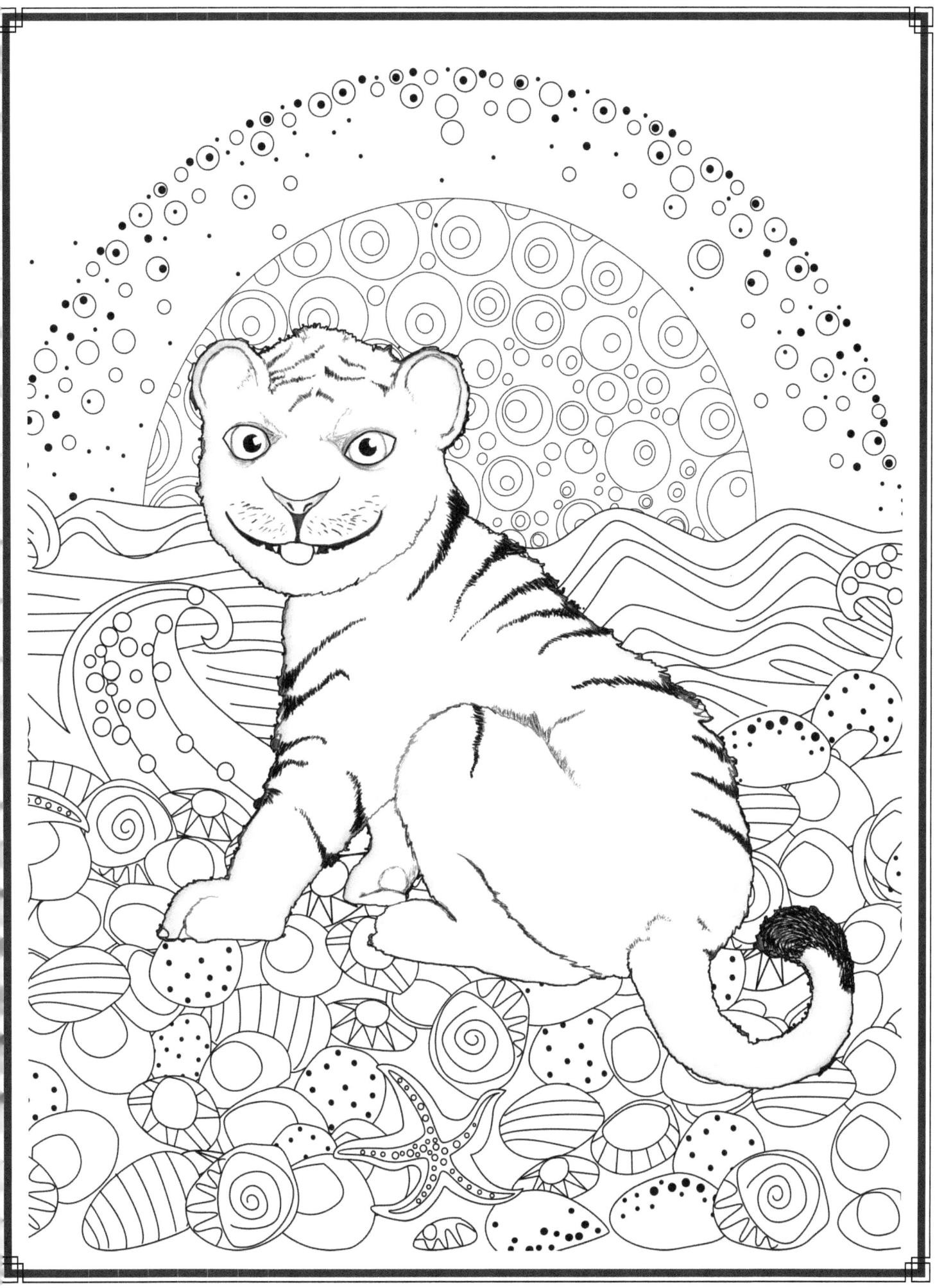

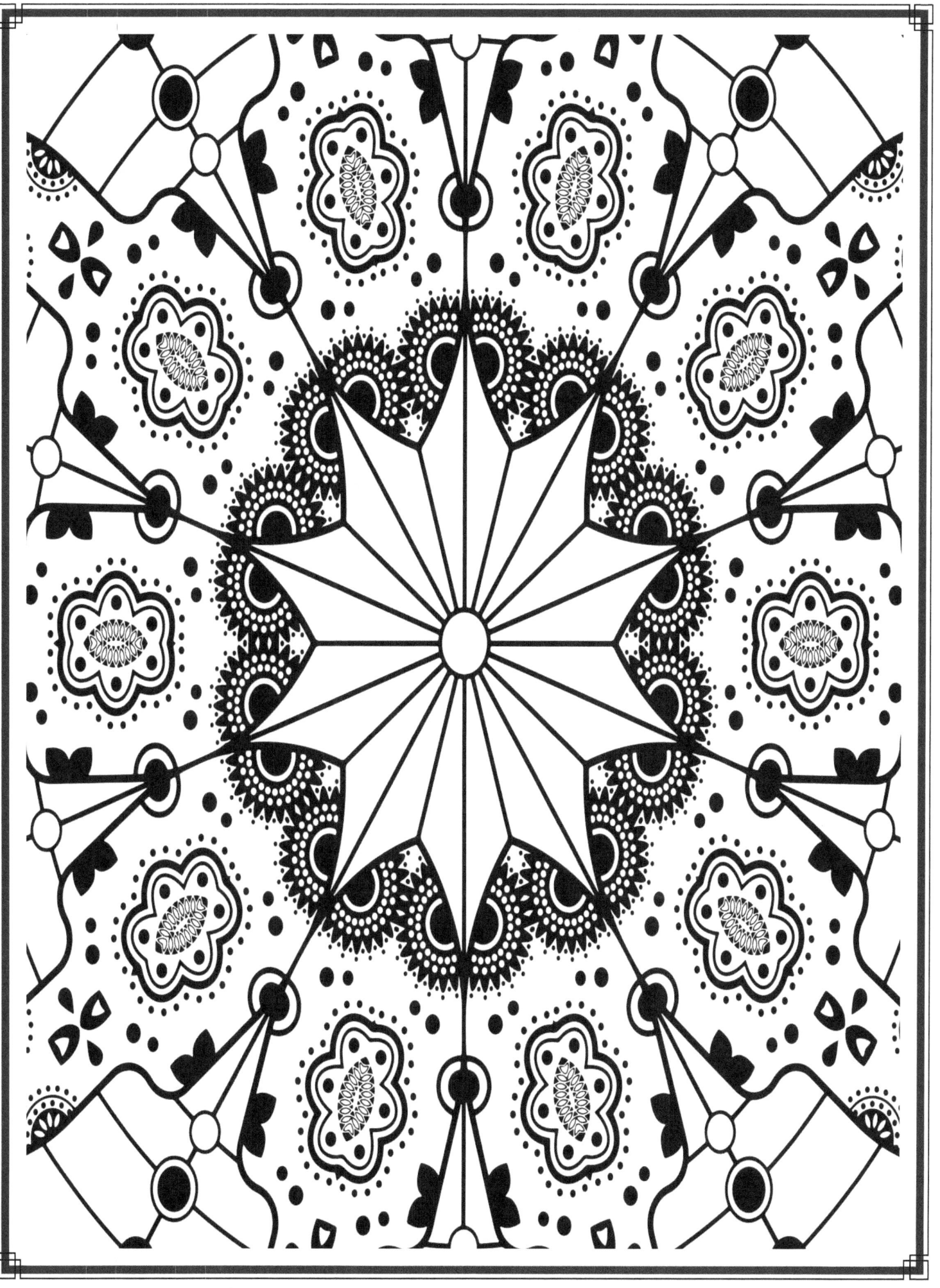

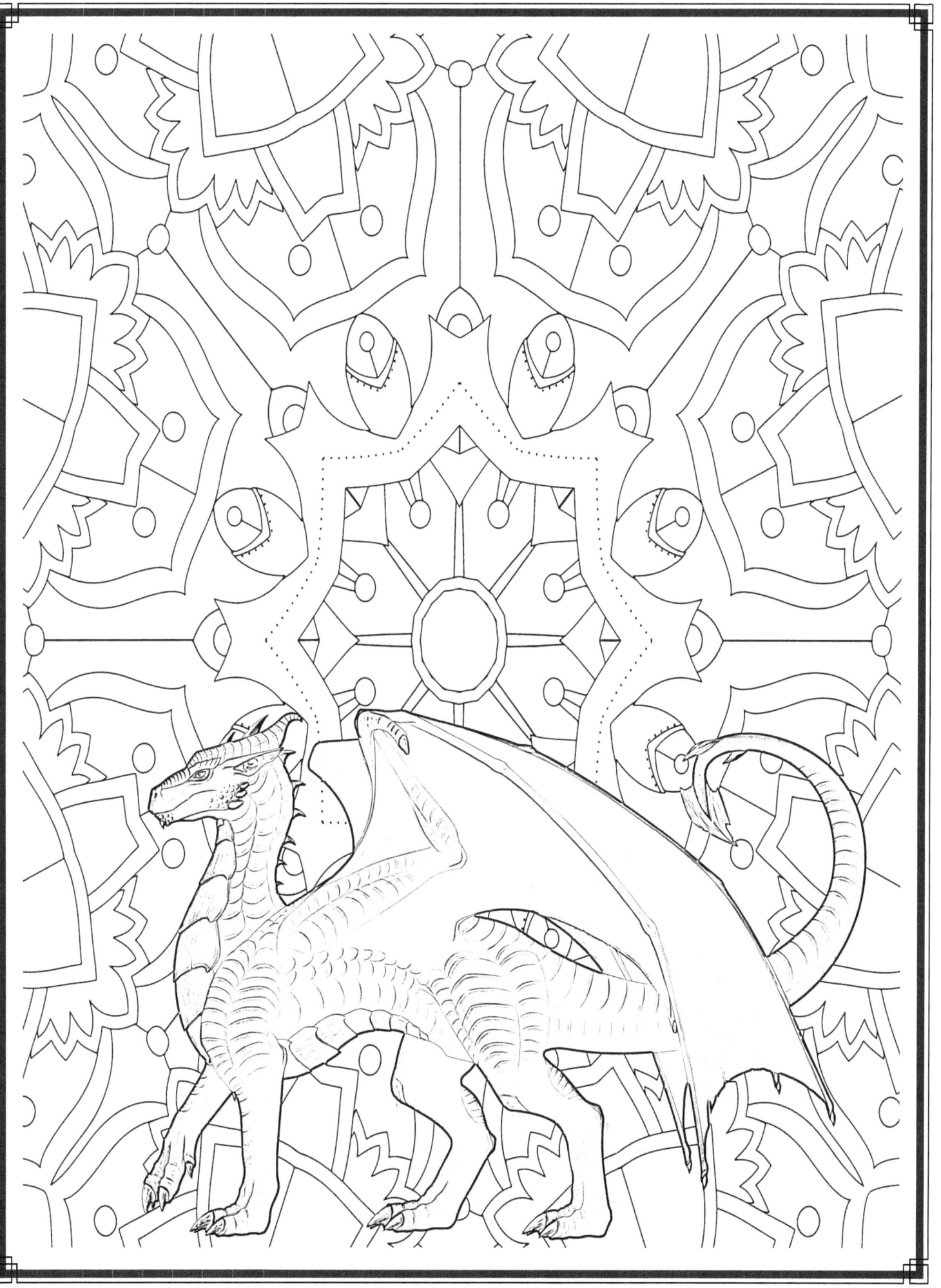

Additional Books and Information

If you loved this story by me (S.E. Smith) please leave a review!

You can also take a look at additional books and sign up for my newsletter to hear about my latest releases at:

http://sesmithfl.com
http://sesmithya.com

or keep in touch using the following links:

http://sesmithfl.com/?s=newsletter
https://www.facebook.com/se.smith.5
https://twitter.com/sesmithfl
http://www.pinterest.com/sesmithfl/
http://sesmithfl.com/blog/
http://www.sesmithromance.com/forum/

Additional Books by S.E. Smith

Short Stories and Novellas

Dragon Lords of Valdier Novella
For the Love of Tia (Book 4.1)

Dragonlings of Valdier Novellas
A Dragonling's Easter
A Dragonling's Haunted Halloween
A Dragonling's Magical Christmas
Night of the Demented Symbiots (Halloween 2)

The Dragonlings' Very Special Valentine

Pets in Space Anthology
A Mate for Matrix

Marastin Dow Warriors Short Story
A Warrior's Heart

Lords of Kassis Novella
Rescuing Mattie (Book 3.1)

The Fairy Tale Novella
The Beast Prince
*Free Audiobook of The Beast Prince is available:
https://soundcloud.com/sesmithfl/sets/the-beast-prince-the-fairy-tale-series

Boxsets / Bundles

Dragon Lords of Valdier Boxset Books 1-3
The Alliance Boxset Books 1-3

Science Fiction Romance / Paranormal Novels

Cosmos' Gateway Series
Tink's Neverland (Book 1)
Hannah's Warrior (Book 2)
Tansy's Titan (Book 3)
Cosmos' Promise (Book 4)
Merrick's Maiden (Book 5)

Curizan Warrior Series
Ha'ven's Song (Book 1)

Dragon Lords of Valdier Series

Abducting Abby (Book 1)
Capturing Cara (Book 2)
Tracking Trisha (Book 3)
Ambushing Ariel (Book 4)
Cornering Carmen (Book 5)
Paul's Pursuit (Book 6)
Twin Dragons (Book 7)
Jaguin's Love (Book 8)
The Old Dragon of the Mountain's Christmas (Book 9)

Lords of Kassis Series
River's Run (Book 1)
Star's Storm (Book 2)
Jo's Journey (Book 3)
Ristéard's Unwilling Empress (Book 4)

Magic, New Mexico Series
Touch of Frost (Book 1)
Taking on Tory (Book 2)

Sarafin Warriors Series
Choosing Riley (Book 1)
Viper's Defiant Mate (Book 2)

The Alliance Series
Hunter's Claim (Book 1)
Razor's Traitorous Heart (Book 2)
Dagger's Hope (Book 3)
Challenging Saber (Book 4)
Destin's Hold (Book 5)

Zion Warriors Series
Gracie's Touch (Book 1)
Krac's Firebrand (Book 2)

Paranormal / Time Travel Romance Novels

Spirit Pass Series
Indiana Wild (Book 1)
Spirit Warrior (Book 2)

Second Chance Series
Lily's Cowboys (Book 1)
Touching Rune (Book 2)

Paranormal Novels

More Than Human Series
Ella and the Beast (Book 1)

Science Fiction / Action Adventure Novels

Project Gliese 581G Series
Command Decision (Book 1)
First Awakenings (Book 2)

Young Adult Novels

Breaking Free Series
Voyage of the Defiance (Book 1)
Capture of the Defiance (Book 2)

The Dust Series
Dust: Before and After (Book 1)

Recommended Reading Order Lists:
http://sesmithfl.com/reading-list-by-events/
http://sesmithfl.com/reading-list-by-series/

Word Search: Dragonlings of Valdier (Solution)

```
R + + + S + G + + + + + + + + + + + R J + + + V
E + + + U + + N Y + + + G + + + + + + A I A + A +
I + + + O + + + I L + N S P A C E + D + L B L + H
D + + + I + + + + N I + + + + + + E + I + E A + O
L + + + C + + + + T N M + S + + + + C + N S + J P
A + + + E + + + F J + U A + Y + R E + T O E + + E
V + A + R + + I + O + + R F + M + E I + I T + + +
+ + + I P + H + + U + + + + + + B N T + B A + + +
+ + + + K S + + + R S + + + + E A + H + M + + +
+ + + + + A + + + N P + + + + S + + + + G + + + +
R E B M A + T + + E R A D V E N T U R E S U + + Y
+ + + + + + + E + Y I B + + + + + + + + + + A E B
A L I E N S + + R + N M A P X I N E O H P + V L A
S A M T S I R H C I G + A B + + + I + + + R E + L
+ + + + + + + + + + N R + O I + + D + + A L P + I
+ F S Y M B I O T S E A D + R E + L + H I I + + N
+ R + + + + + + + N + A + + + S O + M H + + + T
+ I + + + + + T + N E V O L + + G S S + + + + +
+ E G + + + + + S + G + + + + + + + P R + + + + +
+ N + O + + + R E T S A E + + + + A L + + + + + +
+ D + + D + + R + + + + + + + + W + + A + + + +
+ S + + + D + + + + + + + + + + + + + N + + + +
+ H + + + + E + + + + + + + + + + + + + E + + +
+ I + + + + + S + + + + + + H U M A N S T + +
+ P + + + + + S + + + + + + + + + + + + + + +
```

(Over,Down,Direction)
ADVENTURES(12,11,E)
AIKATERINA(3,7,SE)
ALICE(22,2,SW)
ALIENS(1,13,E)
AMBER(5,11,W)
BABIES(12,12,SE)
BALINT(25,12,S)
BIO(21,8,N)
CHRISTMAS(9,14,W)
DANGER(13,16,SW)
EASTER(13,20,W)
FAMILY(14,7,NW)
FRIENDSHIP(2,16,S)
GODDESS(3,19,SE)
GOLDIE(18,18,N)
HARVEY(20,16,NE)
HOPE(25,3,S)
HUMANS(17,24,E)
JABIR(24,5,NW)
JADE(21,1,SW)
JOURNEY(10,6,S)
LAUGHTER(24,13,NW)
LOVE(15,18,W)
MATES(22,9,N)
PARENTS(14,13,SW)
PHOENIX(21,13,W)
PLANET(18,19,SE)
PRECIOUS(5,8,N)
ROAM(15,16,NW)
RUNNING(13,7,NW)
SHIFTING(6,9,NE)
SMILE(19,18,NE)
SPACE(13,3,E)
SPRING(11,9,S)
SYMBA(14,5,SE)
SYMBIOTS(3,16,E)
VALDIER(1,7,N)
VALENTINES(25,1,SW)
WARSHIP(17,21,NE)

Dragon's Ball Pit (Solution)

```
G + + + + + + + + + + + + + + + + + + + + + + + E + + +
+ N + + + + + + + + + + + + + + S K O O B F + + + +
+ + I + + + + + + + + + + + + + + + + + I + + + +
+ + + H + + + + + + + + + + + + + + N + + + + + +
+ + + + C + + + + + + + + + + + K + + + + + + + +
+ + + + + R + + + + + + + + + + + R + + + + + + +
C A F E + + A + + + C O L O R E D E N + + + + + +
+ + + + + + + E + + + F + + + + P + + U + + + T +
+ + + + + + + + S + + + A + + A + + + + R + I + +
D E T S I W T R E L O N + S I + E + + B + P + G +
+ + + + + + + + + + O + + + D T + T + A + L + R +
+ + + + + + + + + + S + + + + + A L + L + U + + +
+ + + + + + + + + + T + + + + + L + A + N + + + +
+ + + + + + + + D C + + + + + S O B + T + + + + +
+ + + + + + + + R + O + + + + + C D E + + + + + +
+ + + + E D A J A + + L + + + + O D N + + + + + +
+ + + + E + + + G + + + R + + B H + + U + + D + +
R + + + F + + + O + + + I R + C M + + O + E + P
+ E + + F + + + N + + C E N + + + A + + F L + U
+ + I + O + + + L + + A A + + G + + + R + + I R S
+ + + D C + + + I + R K + + + + + + + + K + G E H
+ + + + L + + + N A F S R E T H G U A D + E H B E
+ + + + + A + + G A + + + + + + + + + + + + T M D
+ + + + + + V + S + + + + + + + + + + + + + + A +
+ + + + + + + T + + + + + + + + + + + + + + + + +
```

```
(Over,Down,Directi      COFFEE(5,21,N)          JADE(8,16,W)
on)                     COLORED(11,7,E)         KNIFE(18,5,NE)
AMBER(24,24,N)          COLRING(10,14,SE)       LOST(10,10,S)
BALLPIT(18,14,NE)       DAUGHTERS(20,22,W)      MARKET(18,18,SE)
BALLS(20,10,SW)         DELIGHT(23,17,S)        PUSHED(25,18,S)
BOOKS(20,2,W)           DIAPER(14,11,NE)        RUN(21,9,NW)
BREAKFAST(16,17,SW      DRAGONLINGS(9,14,S      SEARCHING(9,9,NW)
)                       )                       TRELON(7,10,E)
CAFE(1,7,E)             FAST(12,8,SE)           TWISTED(7,10,W)
CARA(13,19,SW)          FOUND(22,19,NW)         VALDIER(7,24,NW)
CHOCOLATE(17,18,N)      GRUNTED(24,10,SW)
```

Missing Number Solution

6	×	8	−	9	39
/		−		×	
2	−	1	×	5	−3
+		×		−	
4	−	7	+	3	0
7		1		42	

Hidden Phrase Solution

He watched as the tiny golden dragons took off through the crowd.

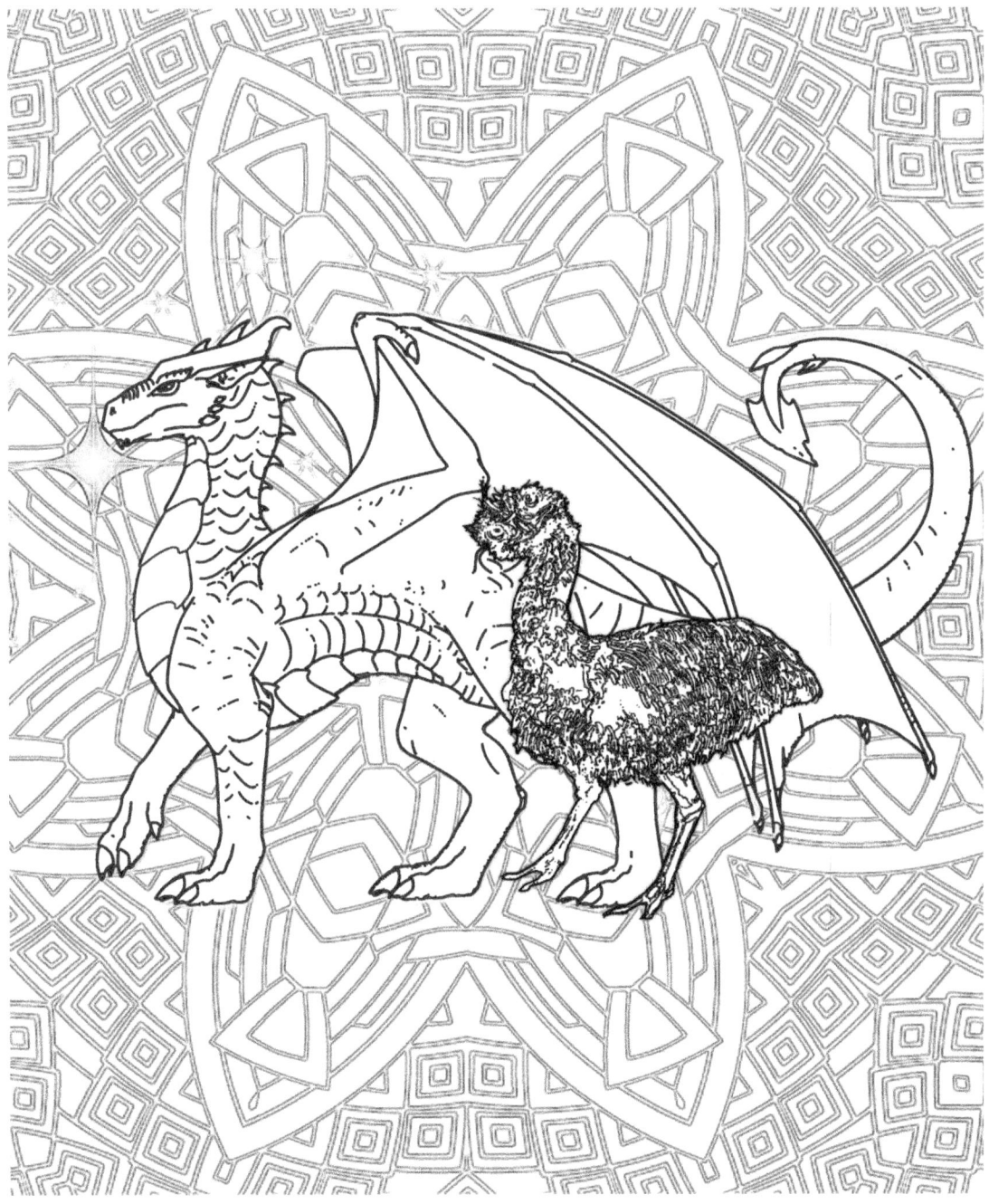

Word Scramble Solution

LOVE
ADVENTURE
PLANETS
SOLAR SYSTEM
GALAXY
STARS
UNIVERSE
ALIENS
DRAGONLNGS
MATES
PARENTS
FAMILY
HOLIDAYS
STORIES
MOUNTAINS
RIVERS
SYMBIOTS
JADE
AMBER
ROAM
ZOHAR
BALINT
JABIR
PHOENIX
SPRING
ALICE

Phrase: Dragonlings

At the Market Scramble Solution

Two
sets
dark
gold
eyes
peered
disappearing
beneath
colorful
balls
market
toys
cafe
chocolate
breakfast
Phrase: Breakfast for Mom

About the Author

S.E. Smith is a *New York Times, USA TODAY, International, and Award-Winning* Bestselling author of science fiction, romance, fantasy, paranormal, and contemporary works for adults, young adults, and children. She enjoys writing a wide variety of genres that pull her readers into worlds that take them away.

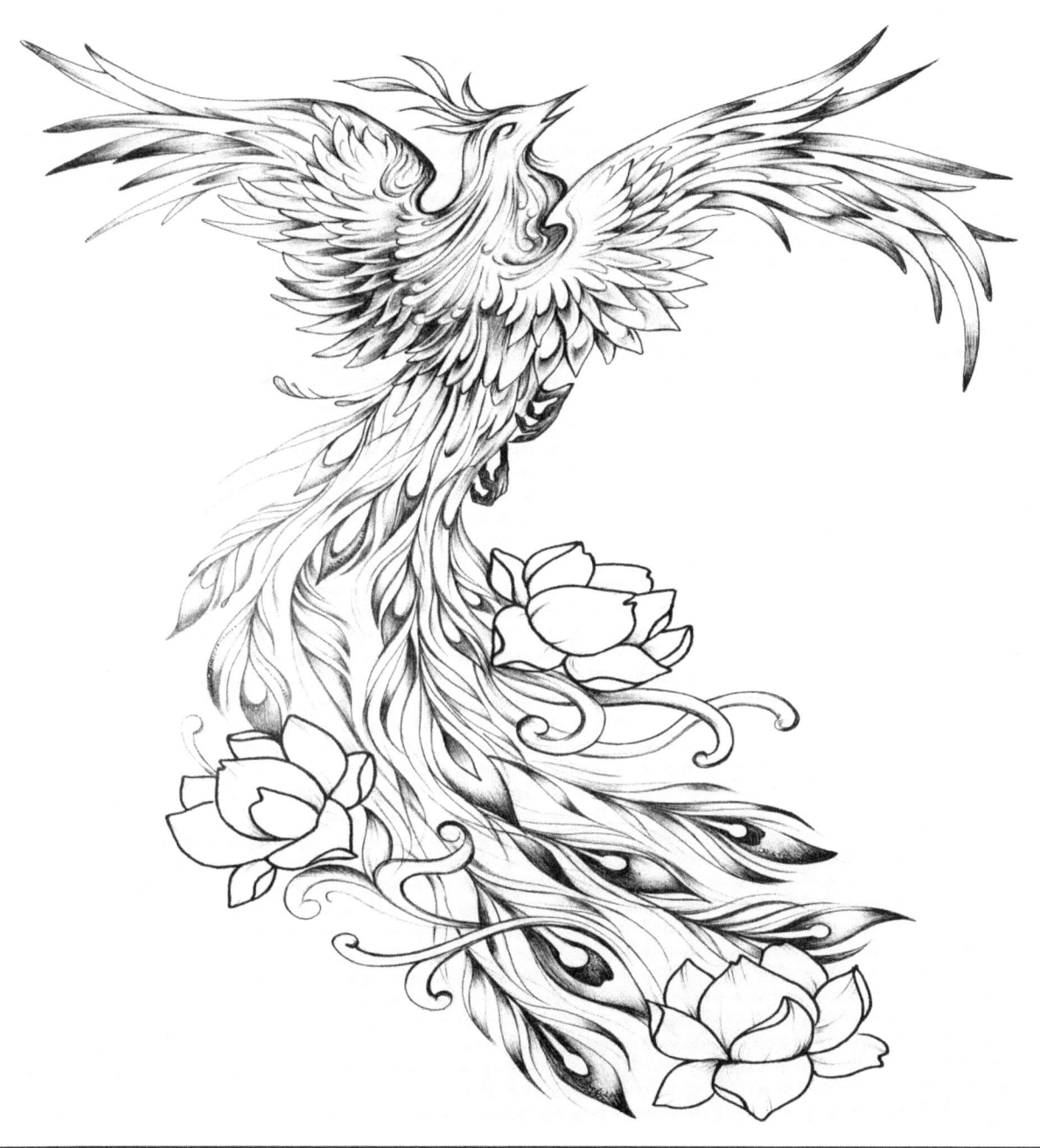

www.ingramcontent.com/pod-product-compliance
Lightning Source LLC
Chambersburg PA
CBHW062215220526
45471CB00009B/3215